"*Apprenticeship with Jesus* is a joy-filled resource for fleshing out the details of ongoing companionship with the Author of our salvation. Putting this book into practice day by day will substantially re-form the inner core of your life."

Richard J. Foster, author, *Celebration of Discipline*

"Gary Moon is a friend, a guide, and fellow apprentice. I know of few people with his passion or his clarity for the subject about which he speaks. I wish every follower of Jesus could have Gary's wisdom on the most important subject in the world—where do we find life?"

John Ortberg, bestselling author; pastor,
Menlo Park Presbyterian Church

"Gary provides wise guidance for our journey toward Christ-likeness that is full of spiritual depth and good humor. What a delightful combination!"

Ruth Haley Barton, president, Transforming Center;
author, *Sacred Rhythms*

"Gary Moon's *Apprenticeship with Jesus* is a well-written book with great stories, practical exercises, and special humor only Gary is capable of, plus deep biblical wisdom on learning to live like Jesus. I highly recommend it for everyone who wants to live as a true disciple of Christ."

Siang-Yang Tan, Fuller Theological Seminary

"Gary Moon's book is perfect for people striving to live and love like our Savior. With grace and beauty, Gary captures the wonder of our salvation, the challenge of our discipleship, and the thrill of transformation, and then follows with a practical guide for navigating this lifelong process. This book is a wonderfully practical tool for transformation."

Eric Parks, Monvee co-creator

Apprenticeship
with Jesus

Learning *to Live*
Like *the* Master

GARY W. MOON

BakerBooks
a division of Baker Publishing Group
Grand Rapids, Michigan

© 2009 by Gary W. Moon

Published by Baker Books
a division of Baker Publishing Group
P.O. Box 6287, Grand Rapids, MI 49516-6287
www.bakerbooks.com

Printed in the United States of America

Library of Congress Cataloging-in-Publication Data
Moon, Gary W., 1956–
    Apprenticeship with Jesus : learning to live like the Master / Gary W. Moon ; foreword by Dallas Willard.
        p.   cm.
    Includes bibliographical references.
    ISBN 978-0-8010-6841-6 (pbk.)
    1. Spirituality. 2. Spiritual life—Christianity. 3. Christian life. I. Title.
BV4501.3.M649 2009
    248.4—dc22   2009018401

Published in association with Eames Literary Services, LLC, Nashville, TN.

Microsoft® Office Outlook® 2007 screenshots reprinted with permission from Microsoft Corporation.

This book is dedicated to my father,
Rev. W. D. Moon,
a true apprentice to Jesus.

Contents

Acknowledgments

This book would not have been written without the presence of several people on the planet. First and foremost, there is Dallas Willard. I often refer to Dallas as America's answer to C. S. Lewis; and I rarely speak to a class for more than ten minutes without quoting him. Occasionally I'll even confess that I've never had an original thought; I'm content to rearrange and simplify those of Dallas Willard. But it's not Dallas's mind that has had the biggest impact on me or this book. In an age where it seems that nontransformation has become the accepted Christian norm, Dallas's simple, loving, non-hurried life shines like a beacon of hope. Reading his life has caused me to believe that it is possible to actually become like Jesus.

It would be difficult to overestimate the impact Dallas Willard has had and will have on the Christian church. It would not surprise me if historians of the late twenty-first century and beyond look back over this period of church history and conclude that the reforming contributions of Dallas Willard should be considered as important as those of Martin Luther and Saint Ignatius of Loyola. Clearly, he has ignited a reformation in thinking that it is possible to actually become like Jesus.

It would also be difficult to overestimate the breadth of Dallas Willard's present influence on young and not-so-young ministers, academics, and lay pilgrims. Two years ago I was attending my first Renovaré board meeting in Colorado as an invited guest. Within five minutes of arriving I met James Bryan Smith for the first time. Within ten minutes we discovered that we both had the same Myers-Briggs profile (I'll spare you the letters). Within fifteen minutes we were shocked to learn that we had both been inspired by Dallas Willard to develop a "Curriculum of Christlikeness" and were working on a book based on the idea of living out an apprenticeship with Jesus. At that point we quickly stopped talking and bolted back to our rooms to see who could get this book finished first. No, that's not true, but we did realize a little more about just how far-reaching and inspirational Dallas's words are to so many.

There are several other people I would like to acknowledge. Charlie Shedd. You are in heaven now, so I'm not sure if you'll see this, but thanks for taking the time to let me be your writing apprentice for a couple of years. John Eames. Thanks for being a wonderful agent and friend and for tricking the folks at Baker into publishing this book. And speaking of Baker, thank you, Chad Allen, for accepting this manuscript and for making it much better; and Barb Barnes, thank you for all the catches and fixes that make it seem like I passed my English classes.

I also want to thank Rich Cannon for investing his extremely valuable time to add a few additions to this book for those who may want to experiment with turning the exercises into something of an E-Rule of life. If this last sentence about E-something doesn't make any sense to you, I'd suggest you skip the E-Rule boxes in the book.

Finally, I want to acknowledge some very special people who made it possible for me to find the time to write this book. Jeff Terrell and Greg Hearn, you are very understanding and supportive bosses. Regina, Jesse, and Jenna Moon, thank you each for your understanding, your support, and your love.

Foreword

This book makes accessible a new vision of life redeemed—bought back—from the pawn shop run by the world, the flesh, and the devil: redeemed through a living, interactive relationship with Jesus Christ. As Gary acknowledges, it is "new" only in relationship to recent practice, and as "old" as the people of Christ.

The action takes place where redemption must take place, in the ordinary life that everyone must live, no matter what kind of "shows" may be running. The author makes clear how anyone and everyone can "take hold of that life which is life indeed" (2 Tim. 6:19). Starting right where they are, they can begin to do simple things that allow the water of spiritual life in Christ to surge through inner and outer channels parched from living "with no hope and without God in the world" (Eph. 2:12).

Discipleship ("Apprenticeship") to Christ is the *status* within which the *process* of spiritual formation in Christlikeness runs its course. The result is "growth in the grace and knowledge of our Lord and Savior Jesus Christ" (2 Peter 3:18). That is the normal Christian life. As his apprentices in Kingdom living and acting, we are with him learning to be like

13

him. That is the general idea. It is what *trusting Christ* means. You cannot actually trust him and fail to be his disciple—no doubt, for a while, a green and bumbling disciple—though currently there is a great deal of deadly misinformation on this point. Trusting Jesus Christ means you want to be with him as much as possible.

A part of our lessons as his students will deal with how we can effectively be together with our Dear Maestro. Gary Moon here makes available an incredible amount of wisdom on that point. He eliminates a lot of holy nonsense that tends to accumulate around "spiritual formation." His down-to-earth stories and impish humor help us stay honest with who and what we are, right in the midst of the supernal drama of redemption in which we share. He does not create a new cloud of words and rituals within which we remain basically unchanged. He does not mistake profession of belief for belief itself.

Belief puts us into action and makes contact with reality. There is much talk today about the failure of belief to govern life. The obvious failures of Christian living are attributed to the weakness of belief. But this has come about because of a growing misunderstanding of "belief," adapted to the prevailing forms of Christianity. We have to adjust "belief" so that *nominal* "Christians" can still "have faith." Those forms of Christianity run on *profession of belief*, and profession of belief is *not* belief. People continue to act in terms of what they really do believe, not in terms of what they profess to believe. They have no other choice. With only minor adjustments here and there, we *always* live up to our beliefs, though rarely up to what we profess.

We grow in genuine faith in Christ as we *put into practice* what little faith we have—from "faith to faith," as we are told (Rom. 1:17). "Mustard seed faith" (Luke 17:6) is so powerful because it grows, not because it acts like a magic potion. The passage here in Luke is about the *increase* of faith (see v. 5). The kingdom of the heavens is like the mustard seed because it *grows* in us and around us (Matt. 13:32; Mark 4:30–32). Effectual instruction in the spiritual life in Christ gives guidelines for putting into practice, right where we are, what little faith we have. For example, we may have a little faith—interwoven with a lot of profession, perhaps—in the Bible. This is commonly the case. We *could* put that faith into practice by memorizing select portions of the Scripture, in the manner this book describes. Then we will certainly experience the reality of the written Word of God, and of the Kingdom in which it dwells. Our beliefs will grow accordingly and our actions will follow.

The book is laid out as a thirty-day journey. That is a good plan. But to enter on the journey, you need to give the book at least one continuous reading. Pick an afternoon and evening when you can concentrate, and *read it from beginning to end.* You need the total impact, which cannot be gained otherwise. And then arrange your affairs where you can seriously do the day-by-day. You will need appropriate times, for you have to *actually do* the exercises set for you. Apprenticeship is not a spectator sport. The exercises are not things you can do and then get on with your "real business"—like "quiet time" as often practiced. They are an indispensable part of your real business, and they help you to know and to engage with what your real business is. It is life with Jesus in the Kingdom of the Heavens.

Dallas Willard

Introduction

Who Would I Be If Jesus Were Living His Life through Me?

[God] offers life, but we must choose to live. This is a far different thing than choosing to be "saved" or accepting "salvation." This is no matter of mere belief but a description of how one lives.

—George MacDonald

Do you ever wonder why it's so difficult to actually do what Jesus would do? Do you ever question if transformation is possible, or if all the Christian talk about abundant life is just gas? I sure have.

As Christians we are supposed to represent Christ to the world, but according to the comprehensive research presented by David Kinnaman and Gabe Lyons in *unChristian*, something is terribly wrong.[1] Christianity has a major image problem—especially among those in the 16 to 29 age bracket—in large part because of the lack of authentic transformation in the lives of people wearing the label "Christian."

Dallas Willard has taken a close look at this elephant of nontransformation in the sanctuary. According to him, "Christianity can only succeed as a guide for current humanity if it does two things: 1) take the need for human transformation as seriously as do modern revolutionary movements, and 2) clarify and exemplify realistic methods of human transformation." He adds, "My central claim is that we *can* become like Christ by doing one thing—following him in the overall style of life he chose for himself."[2] We become like Jesus by learning to live as his "apprentices," learning how to live in light of the fact that we will never stop living.[3]

But we have a major problem. There are two very different "stories" about our relationship to God that have been told across the centuries—one that attracts apprentices and one that repels them.

The Importance of Story

Story is the most powerful invention in the world—and the best way to provide a new vision. With three chords and fifty words a singer can change the way people see a war. With a few indelible parables Jesus illuminated his kingdom and set off a revolution. Story is invasive, relentless like cactus and kudzu; it can root itself in a human heart and push upward, dislodging hard places like broken asphalt.

I learned about stories from my nanny. I called my nanny "Auntie" because Pentecostal preachers' families didn't know about words like "nanny." She was a retired missionary who had spent a lot of time working with thrown-away children in orphanages. Auntie had an oval face, white hair that once was blond, and light blue eyes that were very kind. She loved to tell stories.

I remember that the four years she kept me were before the time poor families could afford television sets. And I remember that it didn't matter so much, because she loved to fill the airwaves with her own images. My first four years of life were lit by her yarns, legends, and fairy tales. I spent my preschool days with stories dancing in my head as Auntie snuggled me in her lap while we rocked together in a creaking chair or swung on the front porch.

During its time as soft clay, my mind was molded by stories. Through no merit of my own, I've become an accidental connoisseur of characters and plots, conflicts and resolution, everything from opening lines to denouement. I know when I hear a bad story as instinctively, I think, as a person whose baby brain was soaked in years of music recognizes a sour note or appreciates one that soars. I know when a story seems well aligned, and I recognize when it wobbles out of balance.

Let me tell you the two stories that have had the biggest impact on my life—and, perhaps, on the entire Christian church. Each presents a very different vision of what is, from the human perspective, the most important concept in Christianity.

Two Visions of Salvation

The First Story

In the first story God creates two naked people without belly buttons and places them in a garden. It's not real clear why he does this, but there is good news—they are naked (I may have already mentioned that) and their primary job is to be fruitful and multiply.

One day while taking a break from multiplying and naming the animals, the woman, influenced by a talking snake, tricks the man into taking a bite from an apple, and all hell breaks loose. God is surprised and then becomes extremely angry. He curses them, every dog, cat, rock, leaf, and Chicago Cubs fan—the entire universe and each of the seven billion-plus and counting descendants who will follow.

Through many millennia God stews in his wrath. He does write down a few instructions and occasionally sends a plague, prophet, or flood to keep folks in line. But mostly he just sits around on a throne, looking a lot like Charlton Heston, and scowls down through the glass-bottom floor of heaven as he thinks up new ways to make humans behave. Then finally, when he can take it no more, he sends his own Son to be tortured and then brutally murdered.

While there are a lot of theories about why God's Son had to die, the bottom line is, it somehow caused God to feel a whole lot better about things and helped him to decide that anyone who hears about what Jesus did and says a magic phrase will once again get to live forever and enjoy paradise. And for those who don't say the incantation? They will burn in flames for all eternity. Don't say the right words and your fate will be a more grotesque horror than what could be conjured up by a committee comprised of Nero, a Salem Witch Trial judge, Hitler, and Ghengis Khan.

I never liked this story.

Story Number Two

In the second story God exists as a loving community of three whose relationship is so joyful, pulsating, and vibrant that it has best been described as a dance.

God decides that this is all too wonderful to keep to himself. So he creates an entire universe and tenderly places humanity at the center, like the offspring of proud parents brought home to a nursery.

Then God does something even more amazing. He plants within the human heart a small but glorious piece of himself. Under his watchful eye these two creatures are to grow into beings who will become as much like God as possible. They are to join the dance, become partners with the Trinity.

But the very first two make a fatal decision. They decide that they can live unplugged from the Tree of Life—the presence and energy of God—and can, in fact, be God themselves.

God is not surprised—he saw this day coming even as he was knitting them together. You can't surprise someone who lives outside the boundaries of time. And he is not angry. He does, however, become very sad as separation and the reality of free will play out before his eyes.

He sets in motion a series of plans to woo us back home, refusing to give up on his original plan to be a nurturing parent to his precious children, showing them how to grow their character until it mirrors his own.

Through the passing millennia God becomes the prodigal Father, standing by his driveway, straining his neck waiting for his children to come home. He sends cards and letters, patriarchs and prophets with the same message: "Your inheritance is waiting; the promises can still be cashed. Come home, I want to be with you, I want to teach you to dance."

But when it becomes clear that we will not come home for longer than a brief visit, God can wait no longer. He empties himself of divine dignity, and wades into the murk and sits down in the mire alongside his prodigal children—becoming as much like us as possible for a while so that we can learn to be like him forever.

Jesus brings the good news that the doors to the kingdom are open wide and that the Trinity still wants us to join the dance, to become as one with them as they are with each other.

And he inhales death and separation into himself and shows through the gruesome image of crucifixion what it looks like to freely die to all that is separate from the will of God. And then he demonstrates through his resurrection that he knows what he's talking about.

But that's not all. He sends the Holy Spirit with music and a dance chart so that we can learn how to waltz with the Trinity, even now, as we wait for the real party to begin.

I love that story! It makes sense out of the fact that the only time Jesus defines eternal life (see John 17:3), he describes it as entering into a deep, intimate, and transforming friendship with members of the Trinity.

The Impact of Those Stories

I believe that either of these two stories, if planted in a human heart, can burst forth and become so invasive that it can determine which path a person inclined toward Christianity will take in approaching God.

When I envision God as wrathful and capricious and see myself as a sinner in his angry hands, the last thing I want is to be *with* him, to be his apprentice. Instead I become desperate for a system of religion that will make me feel safe—in case he and I are ever in the same room together. My intention is *not* to give my whole self in complete surrender, but to look for legal loopholes which will allow me to hold on to as much of my kingdom as possible—while obligating him to let me in on the eternal life benefit. Spiritual disciplines are often seen as a boring, dusty collection of things I can do to win God's favor—or more things to not do and feel guilty about.

But when I re-vision salvation with images from the second story? It turns things inside out. It makes me crave the possibility of a restored relationship with God, a relationship of mutual delight, loyalty, esteem, and lasting commitment. In a righteous relationship (as opposed to a religion's system of wrath management) it is love that comes to define right behavior toward another.

With the second story I am no longer concerned about controlling God, and I find myself inching toward blissful surrender. The second story makes me want to be with him, learn from him, enter into an apprenticeship with him. Spiritual disciplines become ways of learning from my friend and master craftsman of life and relationship.

Story is powerful. One story of God presents images that turn my heart to stone and fill my head with self-loathing thoughts; the other story expands my heart into a dance hall and causes me to long for the Trinity to teach me the steps to the dance they've been doing since before this world began.

Discipleship as Apprenticeship

If we could travel back across the centuries and plop down in medieval London, we would observe a fascinating and functional program for formation. We would encounter apprentices—young men and women—who had moved out of their natural homes, often in the countryside, and into that of their new master. It's a program of learning that certainly calls to mind Jesus' recruitment of his own twelve apprentices.

The central teachings of both Jesus and Paul underscore God's invitation for us to leave our natural habitat (the world of self-rule) and enter into a whole new realm of existence (the kingdom of God-rule). While Jesus liked to talk about "the kingdom" and Paul preferred to use phrases such as being "in Christ," they were describing the same thing: interactive friendship and obedience to Christ, in which we gradually learn to be more like him by being with him—learning how to stay as close to Christ as branches are to their vine. The whole enterprise looks much more like a classical apprenticeship than our modern programs of decision-driven evangelism and fact-wrapped discipleship.

In addition to becoming part of a whole new family environment, the medieval apprentice was also engulfed by a new and broader world—a bustling shop or store in the midst of a teeming city. The apprentice would sleep in the shop or the house of their master, share meals with a "surrogate family," and spend the daylight hours working by the side of an expert craftsman. Until trust was established, a frightening part of the apprentice's new existence was his total dependence on the one he barely knew but was seeking to imitate, to become.

Apprentices learned their new trade, their new way of living, by mirroring their master. And it is interesting that this plan for gradually learning a craft through experience and imitation was regarded as an *initiation into its mysteries*; an alternative name for the guild was a *mystery* (spelled "mistery").[4]

And the master? Above all else, his purpose was to instruct the apprentice without concealing any trade secrets or holding anything back that would hinder the apprentice from some day becoming a master himself and an active participant in the kingdom of the craft, the guild.[5]

As we can see, the textures of an apprenticeship are much deeper and richer than most modern discipleship paradigms. Apprenticeship did not center on a one-time crisis decision or contain the possibility of only visiting with the master once a week on Sunday mornings. While initiation ceremonies were often involved—and sometimes even held in churches—an apprenticeship centered on immersion in the culture of the master, experientially learning to do what he did through hands-on training.

How This Book Is Designed

The thirty days' readings that follow are inspired by this medieval model of formation, Dallas Willard's use of the word *apprentice* as a "with-God" program for transformation. Each reading is built around a story, reflection, and apprenticeship activity. Collectively they are offered as a monthlong training experience for anyone intrigued by the notion of becoming an apprentice to Jesus. The readings—one for each day in a month—are organized around five progressive themes inspired by the apprenticeship metaphor:

1. Getting Started: A "New" Vision for Salvation (Days 1–4);
2. Meet the Master: Reflections on the Keeper of the Mysteries of a New Life (Days 5–8);
3. Know Yourself: Reflections on Me—Apprentice and Student of the Mysteries (Days 9–12);
4. Ways of Being with the Master: Living Life "With Jesus" (Days 13–22); and
5. Carrying on the Master's Legacy: Jesus Living through Me (Days 23–30).

The attempt here is to provide an experiential program for actualizing the amazing promises of Christ. In each reading you'll find a story or two and probing reflections followed by a hands-on daily task offered to inspire entry into an experiential approach to formation. Whereas many programs for discipleship target your head and body—what you think and do—this one is aimed more for your heart. The following thirty-day program is built around the apprenticeship model as a program for being *with* God as you go through the normal routines of your day.

If we are going to deal with the breakdown of "good enough Christianity," that is, Christianity without transformation, we must also step into and experience the solution, an apprenticeship with Jesus. So with no further introduction, I invite you into a journey of progressive experiences of "being with" Christ as we live our daily lives. I hope for you it will be a journey of actualizing the central teachings of both Jesus and Paul—entrance into an interactive friendship with Christ that looks more like a side-by-side medieval apprenticeship than a modern discipleship program.

I recommend that you read only one reading at a time—perhaps just one each day—and with a journal in hand. During each of the suggested exercises, you may want to write in the margins as you reflect on the stories, the explanations, and your experience. But most importantly, take notes on what you hear whispered to you by the Master as you invite him into more and more moments of your day while asking, "Please teach me how to live well, as your apprentice."

Getting Started

A "New" Vision for Salvation

Chris loved to play Nintendo. In fact, some of his friends called him "The Nintendo Wizard." It had been over a year since anyone had beaten him at one of the Nintendo games he owned.

One Christmas Eve his family and several others had gathered for a daylong celebration. The house was filled with warm conversation and all the smells of Christmas. In the den Chris sat in front of the television, playing Nintendo. Uncles, aunts, and cousins passed unnoticed. He was lost in other worlds, racing through mazes, leaping tall buildings, and slaying dragons.

After about an hour had passed, Chris's little brother decided he wanted a turn. He began to ask—very politely—if he could have a turn. Chris totally ignored the request. The little brother's request became louder. Chris remained lost in the game.

Annoyed, the little brother began to poke Chris with his finger. Chris pushed him away with a flying elbow, his thumbs never losing contact with the controls. But the little brother began pounding Chris on the back; the polite request had become a loud command. "Give it up, Chris, it's my turn!"

Chris got up from the chair and moved closer to the television screen, his nose only inches away from entering the land of Nintendo. He said nothing. His gaze was fixed and he continued to move his thumbs in a blur of motion. Chris's little brother began pounding Chris with both fists as hard as he could. No response. In desperation the little brother began to scream, "Let me play right now!!" as he punched Chris hard at the center of his back.

Without stopping the game, Chris turned and shot a glaring look at his little brother. Chris's face was streaked with tears from the pain of being pummeled. "You don't understand!" Chris shouted. "I'm a Nintendo player. It's who I am and it's what I do!"[1]

When I first heard this story, I remember asking myself if there was anything I identified with to that extent. The answer was no. While I'm not saying Chris didn't need a bucket of Ritalin and two shots of discipline, I realize he had a cause for living and he was completely devoted to mastering the craft of Nintendo. He was no casual player.

In the first four readings of this book we'll consider what shifts in spiritual worldview it might take to move beyond being a casual Christian, to being able to say with solemn resolve, "I'm an apprentice of Jesus. It's who I am and what I do!"

What is proposed in this first section will be, for many, nothing short of a "new" vision of salvation.

1

A Case of Theological Malpractice

Salvation Is Also a Life

The whole purpose for which we exist is to be thus taken into the life of God. Wrong ideas about what that life is will make it harder.

—C. S. Lewis

What if the best one-word description of God is "love"? What if love motivated God to appear among us, as one of us, to show us how to live without hurry, fear, or anger? And what if God is still among us, still offering to teach anyone willing to sign on as an apprentice?

But what if, as easy as that sounds, this simple divine intention has been roundly misunderstood and translated into forensic language about appeasement of divine wrath, judgment, substitution, and pardon, exaggerating one profound truth at the expense of another?

A Case of Theological Malpractice

Have you ever been "saved"? Do you remember when it happened? I sure do. I can even tell you about the sermon and who preached it.

I got saved in a little church that was so far out in the country you would have to drive back toward town if you wanted to hunt. Rev. Thurman was preaching a revival, and it was a big one. I think there was someone sitting on each of the twelve pews.

And speaking of big, Rev. Thurman was enormous, a small mountain with suspenders. I remember his suspenders, because he took off his coat as soon as he got behind the pulpit—and they were the first pair I had ever seen. The gust of wind from tossing his jacket over the altar caused Bibles to rustle like fall leaves.

Rev. Thurman had been brought in to our little church as a salvation specialist. He was the type of preacher who told a lot of scary stories about hell and some of the tortured souls who lived there. And he personally knew some who had recently been set ablaze. According to him, they had heard him preach in the past but didn't listen to his warnings and then went out and got themselves killed in car crashes or by lightning bolts.

The imagery was gruesome. But to make a long story short, Rev. Thurman scared the hell out of me. When he gave the invitation, I darted down front and asked Jesus to forgive all my sins—even though as a five-year-old I couldn't recall very many—and I asked God not to make me a rotisserie item in the afterlife.

Then I went back and sat down. I remember that it felt real good and that my parents seemed very happy. Somehow by walking down front I had made God feel a lot better about the huge pile of wrath my sins had caused him to store up. I also remember feeling very guilty that I had caused Jesus so much pain and suffering.

Years passed, and while no one ever showed me a contract or a plan for being a good Christian, I began to put things together on my own. From Sunday school lessons and a parade of preachers, I knew I was supposed to stay away from whiskey, cigarettes, and wild women—including their pictures. And I should be at church whenever it wasn't locked up and give God a significant cut of my money. It also seemed very important to read straight through a King James Bible every year, although personally, I never got past Leviticus without setting it aside for several months, feeling really guilty, and then skipping ahead to John. I also knew you were a better Christian if your Bible was all marked up and if you were the first to locate a verse whenever a preacher called out its address.

More years passed. Adolescence hit. My sins became more obvious to me—but still mostly a secret to others. Each moral failure brought shame, guilt, and white-knuckled determination to do better, to be perfect—starting the very next new day and especially with every New Year. Prayer remained a one-sided conversation with the invisible—usually beginning with "I'm sorry" and ending with "Amen."

I was a Christian, a miserable but forgiven sinner who had a legal and binding contract with God. But except for the "get out of hell free card" that Rev. Thurman told me God had put in my back pocket, I didn't feel or act much different from the heathen. I just kept it a secret.

Ancients and Amateurs

Eventually adulthood arrived. But even with a seminary education and the ability to parse a few Greek verbs, I remained puzzled about just what God had in mind with this "salvation" business. Surely he hadn't come to die so folks could live as tortured souls like me.

Privately, I became pretty cynical about the whole thing. When survey after survey appeared suggesting that Christians looked a whole lot more like non-Christians than Jesus, I wasn't at all surprised. While neither Gallup nor Barna collected any information from my soul, I was sure its dimensions would have fit right in with their sobering conclusions.

But then two important sources of information began coming to my attention with increasing regularity. With each encounter I noticed that a little hope would bubble up in my heart. One spring came from the ideas and writings of ancient Christians and the other from a few amateur theologians.

In my early thirties I started collecting friends who knew a great deal about ancient Christianity. Some even dressed up in black robes on Sundays and walked through their small congregations chanting and swinging incense. Over coffee and baklava, Gyros and cigars, they told me that the Western church had been influenced strongly by Roman law and imperial rule. Because of this, themes such as "God's sovereign rule" and the believer's "legal standing" before him as a pardoned sinner began to predominate salvation thinking across the centuries.

They also shared that, on the other hand, the Eastern church—you know, the side that stayed away from the Crusades, the Inquisition, and televangelism—has always tended to ponder things with their right brains. To them, grace was not so much about a legal release from guilt but the real possibility of a spiritual oneness with God.

Even so, the cultural chasm between the ways and customs of these modern-ancients I was encountering and my own culture was so wide, I'm not sure I would ever have been willing to make the leap to a more romantic and less forensic view of salvation, except for the discovery and rediscovery of writings by some amateur theologians—such as C. S. Lewis, George McDonald, and Dallas Willard—who seemed to be saying some strikingly similar things without causing evangelicals to raise an eyebrow or two.

Reflection
Salvation as a Life

While both the ancient and amateur wisdom I'm referring to will be laced throughout this book, I think it will do for now to say that both these groups—the really old Christians and the recreational theologians—planted a challenging thought in my mind: What if the gospel of justification alone is not enough to generate authentic transformation? What is needed, rather, is to reconsider something as basic as salvation being less about a crisis decision made under duress and more about entering into a "life with God" friendship and apprenticeship for living during which time we drink in grace until it oozes back out our pores.[1]

What if salvation is a life—a way of living each moment of my day with God?

In short, both the ancients and amateurs caused me to believe the best way to think about what I had been calling salvation and discipleship my whole life is actually a journey toward "union in action with the triune God" through entering into an apprenticeship with the Trinity.[2] Being baptized in the name of the Father, Son, and Holy Spirit isn't about getting wet and reverent; it's about emerging into a relationship with the community of God, the Trinity, and learning to live as they do.

Trying to wrap my brain around this caused me to begin wondering aloud with friends, could it really be that spiritual formation can advance until we can say without crossing our fingers, "It is no longer I who live, but it is Christ who lives in me" (Gal. 2:20 NRSV)? I find the lives of the Christians who get this very inspiring—people like Frank Laubach, Mother Teresa, Thomas Kelly, and Dag Hammarskjöld. And if I wanted to peel back a few more years, I'd certainly add Leo Tolstoy, Brother Lawrence, and many others.

What attracts me to each of these individuals is the raw honesty in their writings about dissatisfaction with a form of Christianity which was not working for them—what many of us might call normative Christianity; what Kierkegaard calls "gentle Christianity." I'm drawn to these individuals because they weren't satisfied with the "good enough" versions, and their dissatisfaction became a springboard for a different way to live. For each, the latter chapters of life began to center progressively on a radical reorientation of priorities and a dramatic reinvestment of time in learning to live more and more moments in greater awareness of God and as partners in divine friendship.[3]

With this in mind, our foundational apprenticeship activity will focus on our *Week-at-a-Glance* calendars. Our first "to do" will be to get to our day planners before anyone else can.

pprentice Activity

Get to Your Calendar Before Anyone Else Can

It was a favorite theme of C. S. Lewis that only lazy people work hard. By lazily abdicating the essential work of deciding and directing, establishing values and setting goals, other people do it for us; then we find ourselves frantically, at the last minute, trying to satisfy a half-dozen different demands on our time, none of which is essential to our vocation, to stave off disappointing someone. This theme is perhaps best described by Eugene Peterson: "I am busy because I am lazy. I indolently let others decide what I will do instead of resolutely deciding myself. I let people who do not understand the work of the pastor write the agenda for my day's work because I am too slipshod to write it myself."[4]

So run, don't walk, to your *Outlook* Calendar, *Entourage* Calendar, *Week-at-a-Glance* booklet, *Excel Spreadsheet*, or the napkin on which you scribble your weekly "to-do" list, and block out

1. Eight hours a night for sleeping, and

2. An additional two hours for practicing the two supreme commandments—time for loving God, others, and yourself. Give God your best time, which means different things to morning versus night people.

And here's the deal. The only request is that you try these exercises for thirty days—beginning with today—getting eight hours' sleep and writing God into your schedule each day. See if your life begins to improve. If you don't like the results, throw this book away and move on to another one.

As you are pondering this, perhaps the words of Eugene Peterson will be motivational: "I mark out the times for prayer, for reading, for leisure, for the silence and solitude out of which creative work can issue. I find that when these central needs are met, there is plenty of time for everything else."[5]

▲ Semi-Permanent Insertions in My Week-at-a-Glance Calendar

In case you would like to use Microsoft (MS) Outlook in creating an "E-Rule of Life" with these exercises, we'll offer you some helpful hints. Screenshots for creating an appointment on your calendar are found in the appendix.

1. To create an appointment with yourself for sleeping 8 hours a night, you could do the following:

> In MS Outlook under Calendar, create an appointment for 8 hours of sleep (see appendix table 1). Click Recurrence, insert the Start and End time, select Daily, save the appointment.

2. To insert two hours of time for being with God, you may wish to either

> Schedule a two-hour block by adding a new appointment. Click Recurrence, select 2 hours, repeat Daily, click OK (see appendix tables 2 and 3).

> Schedule shorter time slots by adding several appointments. Click Recurrence, select 30 minutes, repeat Daily, click OK. Repeat for each additional time slot (see appendix table 4).

Getting Beyond Vampire Christianity

Transformation as Transfusion

The assumption of Jesus' program for his people on earth was that they would live their lives as his students and co-laborers.

—Dallas Willard

One of my lifetime goals is to visit every major league baseball park and watch a game while eating as many hot dogs as possible. Once while attending a conference in Chicago, I was able to duck out long enough to see the Chicago Cubs play at Wrigley Field and the White Sox at Comiskey—all on the same day. Now that was a good conference. But my most unforgettable baseball memory occurred while I was watching a junior varsity B-team play on their home field, beside a hog barn in rural Georgia.

In both professional ballparks I was sitting two zip codes from home plate. By the time I *heard* the crack of the bat, the ball was already caught, and the other pitcher was warming up. At the JV game I sat much closer to the action—on the first row, directly behind the catcher. I was close enough to hear him say "Ouch!" and reference his surprising relationship with the leadoff hitter's mother. And if that weren't entertaining enough, each ball fouled to the right caused a herd of pigs to squeal like they were being used as catcher's mitts in an exorcism. That's baseball! You don't get enough of that at Wrigley Field.

The pitcher let go of what was supposed to be a curve ball. But it didn't bend. It left his hand and headed straight for the visiting team's dugout. Everyone hit the deck and then began to point at the pitcher while resting most of their other fingers.

"Ball three," the umpire yelled from eighty feet away. "Outside!"

The pitcher's face turned beet red. Maybe it wouldn't be so easy to get a hit in this league, I reasoned, as the hitter's knees looked a little wobbly. Even the pitcher didn't know where the ball would go.

The catcher signaled for the next pitch to be straight and in the vicinity of home plate. I could tell, because he was pointing at his mitt and cussing.

"Strike three! You're out!" the umpire called after a 40 mph "fast" ball crossed the plate. The hitter had never taken the bat off his shoulder as a ball floated past his trembling knees. He was just glad to be alive.

A hundred pigs sighed in relief.

But the playing field wasn't the only place for action. Fun stuff was happening in the stands too. A man was sitting beside me with his granddaughter on his lap. His youngest son was the opposing team's catcher.

"Hey, Papa," the little girl began, "why do they let vampires on the field?" She looked worried.

Everyone around the child stopped talking. It was like an E. F. Hutton commercial. What did she mean?

"Vampires?" her grandfather questioned. "Honey, there aren't any vampires out there."

"Yes, there are," she said. "You said there were. You said they should 'throw the vampire out,' and that he was blind as a bat. I don't like vampires. They mean."

At that everybody in earshot laughed so loudly it reactivated the pigs.

"Honey, I didn't say 'vampire,'" the grandfather said. "I said 'umpire.' That man standing behind Johnny is the umpire."

"Oh," she said. But she still looked worried.

"Is he a mean one? Will he bite Johnny when he's not looking?"

Reflection

The Way to Transformation Is Transfusion

I can't hear the word *vampire* without thinking about something I heard Dallas Willard say. Dallas believes a serious problem exists in the Christian church. He says it's rare to find anyone who wants so badly to be transformed into the image of Christ that he or she is willing to pay the price for it to happen. This causes Dallas to wonder why the conservatives and liberals fight so much. After all, both groups agree on the main thing. Actually becoming like Jesus is too hard even to try—so let's agree to fight about politics and religion, hymns versus choruses, and stay away from the tough issue: actually becoming like Jesus.

That's where his term *vampire Christians* comes in. Most of us, Dallas muses, take a vampire approach to being a Christian. We want just a little blood for our sins, enough for eternal life, but not a total transfusion of Jesus' life and character. And we certainly don't want to hang around with him all the time.

38

As apprentices, we need to enter into a daily relationship with Jesus that begins with continual conversations and progresses into intimate communion. We need nothing less than a total transfusion of his will, thoughts, emotions, behavior, and social interactions, until we can say with the apostle Paul, "For to me, to live is Christ and to die is gain" (Phil. 1:21).

But I suspect that many of us—if suddenly injected with truth serum—would confess to being vampire Christians. How else can we explain survey after survey which reveal so little difference between professing Christians—even conservative, evangelical Christians—and the "world."

Thanks to Barna and other pollsters, we know that Christians and non-Christians divorce each other at about the same rates (in fact, evangelical Christians recently moved into first place); show a similar rate for domestic violence; and even with all the sermons on tithing, Christians give about 2.6 percent of their income to charitable causes as compared to 2.4 percent for non-Christians. That's right; all those sermons threatening hellfire and brimstone have only resulted in 0.2 percent difference in giving.[1] Amazing!

Even more amazing, the South—my region of the country—known for states being colored red on election day because of conservative views on politics and religion, leads all other regions in Internet spending on pornography.

And, on an even more sobering note, just a few years ago we observed, yet again, that being a prominent religious leader, even a prominent evangelical religious leader, even being *the* leader, does not provide sufficient padding when it comes to the false self kicking the true self in the butt. It's not even a fair fight.

But there is hope. It starts with telling the truth. Christianity that allows and even normalizes vampire approaches to our relationship with Christ is not Christianity at all. Salvation that emphasizes forgiveness of sins over a lifelong journey to union with God is not salvation. And a program of discipleship that is built on anything other than the development of an experiential apprenticeship with Jesus is not worth the flannel it was taught on.

These are strong words, but I'll back them up as we go along. The only way to transformation is through transfusion. And the best way to experience a transfusion of Christ's life and power is to become his apprentice. It's time to throw out the vampire.

Apprentice Activity

Let's Begin by Imitating Some Drunks

Now that you've gotten to your day planner and carved out time for rest and apprentice training, let's take the next crucial step—raw honesty about where we are and the desire for transfusion.

If you'll permit one last Dallas quote for this reading, I'd like to point out that he believes that any program for Christian spiritual formation the church develops, if successful, will look a whole lot like an AA program. And it will begin with raw honesty about our present condition, a surrender of our will to the will of God, and an ongoing transfusion of divine will with accountability to a group and at least one other individual.

For our purposes here, let's begin with a sobering self-assessment—our second apprentice activity. Please take a few moments to consider the following "steps." They closely resemble the 12 Steps of AA but have been modified slightly to become even more appropriate to the journey of becoming more like Jesus.

Make each a confession to Christ. Pause after saying each. Be honest with yourself about whether or not you have actually made this step. Conclude with a prayer for an ongoing transfusion of the will, power, and presence of Christ in your life. While you should complete all twelve confessions, for our purposes at this point, pay particular attention to the first three.

12 Confessions

1. *I admit that I am powerless to fix the brokenness of my life on my own. My life has become unmanageable.*

2. *I believe that God—through his actions and those of his Son Jesus and the Holy Spirit—can restore me to sanity.*

3. *I will turn my will and my entire life over to the care of God. Father, I'm asking for a total transfusion of your will, power, presence, and love.*

4. I will make a searching and fearless inventory of my life to discover all the ways I have engaged in self-worship (by being in control instead of living surrendered to the will of God).

5. I will admit to God, to myself, and to another human being the exact nature of my wrongs.

6. I am entirely ready to have God remove all the defects in my character and replace them—through his presence—with the thoughts, emotions, will, behavior, and relationship patterns of Christ.

7. I humbly ask God to help me become willing to deny myself—and the desire to live life on my terms—and to remove my shortcomings.

8. I will make a list of all the people I have harmed and become willing to make amends.

9. I will make direct amends to all I have injured.

10. I will continue to take personal inventory, and when I wrong someone, I will promptly admit it.

11. I will through prayer, meditation, and the practice of other Christian disciplines attempt to improve my conscious contact with God.

12. Having experienced some measure of authentic transformation as a result of surrendering all aspects of myself to the power and presence of Christ, I will carry this message to others and continue to practice these principles in all my affairs.

▶ *Creating a One-Time-per-Week Prompt*

To use Microsoft Outlook for creating a One-Time-per-Week Prompt for this exercise or any of the following exercises, please follow these steps to be reminded of these "12 Confessions" at least once per week:

Step 1: Create a New Task Item by clicking New, then Task.

Step 2: Put the 12 items into the task list. Change the status to In Progress. Click the Recurrence button and set the reminder to the date and time appropriate.

See screen samples in appendix tables 1–4, which correspond to the steps for creating a recurring weekly reminder, and appendix table 5 with the 12 Confessions.

DAY
3

Why Paul Rarely Quoted Jesus

The Great Mystery Revealed

God has created us for intimate friendship with himself—
both now and forever.

—Dallas Willard

This summer I was vacationing with my family in Europe
when I was slapped in the face by a sentence hiding in a
book. We were near the end of our adventure and had worn
most of the print off our four Eurail passes. My wife and two
daughters were napping, and by reading Huston Smith's *The
World's Religions*, I was trying not to join them. Somewhere
between London and Edinburgh, I found the words that left
me red-faced: "Paul, whose letters epitomize the concerns of
the early Church, knew what Jesus had taught, but he almost
never quotes him."[1]

I was jolted. My first reaction was to question the theological veracity of the author. Surely he must have it wrong. I was aware Paul did not have access to a red-letter New Testament, but I still could not fathom how the individual whom God dramatically called and personally trained for the job of apostle would "almost never" quote the source of the Christian faith. It couldn't be!

When I got home, I immediately emailed a trusted friend and student of Scripture—and namesake of the apostle in question—Paul Smith. I asked him if the claim were true, and within the hour he sent me the only three passages he knew in which Paul quotes Jesus: Acts 20:35; 1 Corinthians 11:23–25; and 2 Corinthians 12:9. When he reminded me about the lack of a good King James Bible in Paul's day, I reminded him that I've quoted Dallas Willard more than three times while standing in the express lane at our grocery.

Jesus was transformational. This fact is perhaps most graphically supported by the two very different lives lived by Saul/Paul, but Huston Smith's observation is poignant: "The news that transformed [Paul] was not Jesus' ethical precepts . . . it was something different."[2] But if not Jesus' words, then what was it that transformed lives, producing men and women who found the secret of living and a willingness to face Roman legions and hungry lions?

And then there is the even tougher question. How can we expect a person who lived over two thousand years ago to produce radical change in a human life here and now?

I believe Lewis Smedes offers the most likely answer to those questions—as well as to why Jesus was infrequently quoted by Paul.[3] According to Smedes, Paul's writings are driven by one consuming theme. One hundred sixty-four times Paul makes reference either to our being "in Christ" or to Christ's being "in" us. Apparently, the apostle believed there was something even more important and transforming than the moral teachings of Jesus. It was the great mystery revealed. It was the present possibility of entering into union

44

with Christ—the center and condition of authentic human existence.

The more I reflected on Huston Smith's observation, the more I became convinced that Paul's central teaching—being "in" Christ—is closely connected to learning to live our lives as his apprentice. To be "in Christ" is to stay connected to him; it is learning to abide with God, to be connected to him as branches are organically connected to the vine as Jesus describes in John 15:1–5:

> I am the true vine, and my Father is the gardener. He cuts off every branch in me that bears no fruit, while every branch that does bear fruit he prunes so that it will be even more fruitful. . . . Remain in me, and I will remain in you. No branch can bear fruit by itself; it must remain in the vine. Neither can you bear fruit unless you remain in me. I am the vine; you are the branches. If a man remains in me and I in him, he will bear much fruit; apart from me you can do nothing.

To be "in Christ" is to live with our souls plugged into the divine love of God and a way of fulfillment of Jesus' prayer in John 17: "I ask . . . that they may all be one. As you, Father, are in me and I am in you, may they also be in us . . . that the love with which you have loved me may be in them."

Perhaps the reason Paul quoted Jesus' words so infrequently was the lead story he was covering at the time: "the mystery that has been kept hidden for ages and generations, but is now disclosed to the saints. . . . Christ in you, the hope of glory" (Col. 1:26–27).

I don't believe the transforming power of Christ is present with us now because he once said, "Love your neighbor as yourself," but because the living Christ can love my neighbor through me by being *in* me. The difference here can be as vast as the chasm that separates reading a prayer *about* God from experiencing prayer *with* God.

Reflection

The Great Mystery Revealed—Christ Within, Being Lived Out

Many have made the case that the most central teaching of Jesus was life in the kingdom of God.[4] Some go so far as to say that while on earth Jesus only did three things. He introduced the kingdom (see Mark 1:15). He taught the ethics of the kingdom—with the Sermon on the Mount being the most concise example. And he demonstrated through performing signs and wonders that he had the right to do such teaching about the availability of a whole new way to live.

But what if the number one teaching point of Jesus and the number one teaching point of Paul are one in the same? They are. The reality of the kingdom is the gospel, the Good News. The kingdom is that realm where the will of the king and the will of a subject are one. Life in the kingdom is a life of interactive friendship with God, the process of learning to be like God, learning to will his will, learning to be with God. Ultimately to be "in" the kingdom is to be "in" Christ. Both Jesus and Paul seemed most passionate about teaching a whole new way to live—intimately and organically connected to Christ, like branches to a vine, like members of the Trinity, a union of love.

A few weeks ago I was sitting in a trendy restaurant in Atlanta called the Flying Biscuit—a strange name, but a much better choice than the Tossed Cookie. I was trying to ingest a tofu barbecue plate and a mountain of salad while my two friends were mauling a pair of large greasy steaks. One friend was a lifelong southern Baptist; the other was Anglican. Both were ordained. Neither offered any parts of his steak, so I couldn't tell who the better Christian was.

At some point in the conversation the Anglican friend made reference to Thomas Merton's autobiography, *The Seven Storey Mountain*. He was trying to explain the rich meaning of the

Eucharist in his spiritual life and brought Thomas Merton's conversion story in to support his case. Even before his "official" conversion, Merton had developed the habit of attending Mass on a daily basis, feeling strangely drawn in by the feelings of intimacy, warmth, and belonging that so often accompanied his participation in the Eucharist.

When my Baptist friend looked a little confused, I stepped into the conversation to interpret. I felt it my duty as someone who speaks both evangelical and sacramental.

"When I experience the Eucharist, Mike, it takes me back to the time 'I got saved'—but without the guilt and fear. When I receive the elements, I most often say the same thing I said when I was five years old—but with a few grown-up words thrown in. I say 'Please be inside me, Jesus, at the very center of my being. Be in every atom in my body, empowering me with your presence, power, and love. I don't know how to live my life, but you do. Live your life through me. Amen.'

"I don't think about any nuances of theological differences," I went on to say. "I don't think about *trans-* or *con*substantiation. I'm just repeating a forty-year-old prayer to be 'in' Christ and for him to be 'in' me."

*A*pprentice Activity

Take Communion Forty Times Today— and Every Day after That

Apparently God is pretty big. Astronomers now believe that bodies in space exist that are over ten billion light-years from here. Theologians believe that God is everywhere—simultaneously at the edge of the universe and right there by your side. God is everywhere and God is love (1 John 4:8). Because of these two realities, there can be a sacred sense in which to breathe is to experience communion with God. Try this:

> Make a list of three things you will definitely be doing a lot over the next twenty-four hours (e.g., taking a drink of water, looking at your watch, sitting at a red light, hugging your spouse or children). Then make a commitment that each of these acts will be a prompt for you to take a twenty-second break from life as usual for a couple of deep, slow breaths.

Things I do a lot:

_____

_____

_____

During these 20-second breaks, say slowly to yourself—and to God:

> [Inhale] "Jesus, I invite you to the center of my being."
> [Exhale] "I don't want to be a Vampire Christian."
> [Inhale] "Christ, I want a total transfusion of your life into my own."
> [Exhale] "Live your life through me."

Choose prompts that will have you participating in this twenty-second communion experience forty or more times a day. (Pairing it with every swallow of a beverage will more than accomplish this goal.)

Note: If you decide to continue this exercise in the future, you may wish to simplify so that the prompting activities become reminders to say:

> [Inhale] "Lord Jesus."
> [Exhale] "Live your life through me."

▶ *Creating a One-Time-per-Day Prompt*

To use Microsoft Outlook for creating a One-Time-per-Day Prompt for this exercise or any of the following exercises (see appendix table 6), please follow these steps:

1. To be reminded of Examine Myself through "Morning Commitments" at least once per day in the beginning of the day:

Step 1: Create a New Task Item by clicking New, then Task.

Step 2: Put the commitment question into the task list as shown. Change the status to In Progress. Click the Recurrence button and click Daily. Finally, set the reminder to the time appropriate, first thing in the morning.

ADDITIONALLY: You can create a nighttime once-per-day prompt in the same way simply by setting the reminder time to the evening.

DAY 4

Becoming Odd for God

The Divine Cultural Exchange Program

A real Christian is an odd number anyway.
—A. W. Tozer

Peter addresses us as "aliens and strangers in the world" (1 Peter 2:11). What a strange thing to say to creatures that bleed red and are standing on planet Earth. If we are not from *here*, then where are we from?

It's not that I can't relate to feeling like an alien. I grew up in a small, slow-paced town, thirty minutes from the nearest movie theater. But during my early twenties through mid-thirties, I lived in the bustling cities of Pasadena and Virginia Beach. During those years it seemed that every time I would open my mouth I dropped fifteen IQ points. It was tough to go from the country to the city. But as I found out later, going back was even tougher.

One morning, not long after moving "back home," I found myself out of bed before the roosters. Deciding to make the best of a bad situation, I dressed for the day and went out for a predawn breakfast.

I arrived at what had been my favorite country eatery, but I noticed something strange this time around. Not only was my car the only Volvo present; it was the only car. Every other vehicle in the parking lot was a truck—pickup trucks, to be precise, twelve of them.

Entering the restaurant, I saw a dozen men huddled around a long table. Each was wearing denim overalls, work boots, and baseball caps that were serving as mini-billboards for farm equipment or chewing tobacco. I think Norman Rockwell would have been unpacking his paints—and then sending out for more blue.

To them I must have looked like a lawyer about to try a case in the Supreme Court—or worse yet, the psychologist that I had become. Before I knew it, I was loosening my silk tie and trying to hide my polished shoes under the table. To say the least, I was feeling out of place—a collie at a bulldog convention.

Just then, one of the twelve slid his chair across the tile floor, sustaining a note just to the right of the keys on a piano. He sauntered to the cash register and paid for his grits out of a wallet that was chained to his overalls. As he walked past, he looked me over with a critical eye. The expression on his face said loud and clear, "*I don't think that boy is from 'round here.*"

No one likes to appear odd. It's so much easier to adopt the customs and appearances of those around us—we take that course in middle school. So for a brief second that morning, I entertained the idea of trading in my Volvo for a pickup truck. And then I considered the situation from the reverse angle. Can you imagine what it would take for me to get one of those pickup fellows to trade in his truck for a Volvo, wear liberal loafers, and discuss Kierkegaard? Images of snowballs in unseasonably warm places came to mind just as the really big thought hit me:

Isn't this precisely what Jesus was up against? He came to earth from a foreign culture to find followers who would be willing to exchange their ways (those of the world) for his (the culture of the kingdom). That cultural exchange program presented a contrast far greater than what exists between the customs of country and city dwellers.

Jesus came to earth looking for folks willing to become odd for God—different from the world—and he still is. It's been a tough sell for almost 2,000 years. If we actually try on such a different way of life, we're going to appear more out of place than a hula skirt at a Mennonite barn raising.

It's so hard to do—to live as if we are not from around here—isn't it? Thank God most churches have the decency to let us off the hook. No need to be a radical. Just pay the monthly premium on your fire insurance policy and blend in. Whew! What a relief. Who wants to be different?

Okay, but what if it is true that our real identity is unceasing spiritual beings and our true home is the kingdom of heaven?[1] What if our main reason for being here is to experience life as a transforming friendship with God, daily learning how to reign and rule with God forever?[2] After all, Jesus' central message did seem to be that our true culture *is* the kingdom and it's time to come back home, right here and now. He's looking for people willing to resist earthly rhythms and begin dancing to a Trinitarian beat.

If this is true, it's going to take more than a one-time crisis to sustain it. It will take an interactive apprenticeship with Jesus where we will begin to feel at home in the realm of our true home.

That is what Christianity is all about.

Reflection

Life in the Kingdom

The two "normal curves" drawn below represent the "world" and the "kingdom." What is "normal" in the world may well appear "abnormal" or "odd" in the kingdom, and vice versa. The primary mission of Jesus—as recorded in Scripture—was to introduce the kingdom and invite folks to enter into that realm and to learn how to approach life in a wholly different manner. Let's consider some of the key differences between what seems normal "here" and "there."

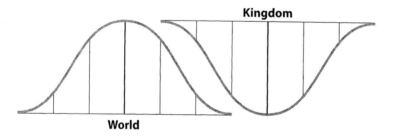

Kingdom

World

What's Normal in Your Culture?

Category	World	Kingdom
Primary Consideration	Me	We
Driving Passion	Fear	Love
Primary Orientation	Pride	Humility
Relationship to God	Distant/Nonexistent	Interactive Friendship
Key Description	Living for Me and Mine	With-God Life
Condition of Heart	Willful/Determined	Willing/Obedient

Apprentice Activity
A Meditation on Being Odd

Take a few moments to reflect on the two cultures presented above and then slowly read Tozer's meditation on becoming odd. Then thank God that you have been invited into the greatest adventure of your life, an apprenticeship for life in the kingdom.

A Meditation by A. W. Tozer
A real Christian is an odd number anyway.
He feels supreme love for one whom he has never seen.
He talks familiarly every day to someone he cannot see,
expects to go to heaven on the virtue of another,
empties himself in order that he might be full,
admits he is wrong so he can be declared right,
goes down in order to get up.
He is strongest when he is weakest,
richest when he is poorest,
and happiest when he feels worst.
He dies so he can live,
forsakes in order to have,
gives away so he can keep,
sees the invisible,
hears the inaudible,
and knows that which passeth knowledge.

...

Father,
Help me to be all you want me to be. No matter how odd I appear to this world. You know me like no one else. You knitted me together in my mother's womb. You want to walk with me, to talk with me, as you did with Adam and Eve. I want this very much. Apart from living my life with you, connected to you like branches in a vine, I can do nothing. But with you all things are possible. Please, as your servant Paul wrote, "let your mind be in me."

Meet the Master

Reflections on the Keeper of the Mysteries of a New Life

In medieval times the master was a person established in a trade or craft and was well respected in the city—as evidenced by membership in the guild. A good master had accepted a series of obligations that regulated his behavior in this quasi-familial pact. He agreed to provide room, board, and clothing for the apprentice and did not ask his young student to perform tasks, such as carrying water, that were for menial servants.[1]

The master desired a close relationship with his apprentice—after all, the young man was a potential guild brother, son-in-law, and even successor to the master's wife and business should the master die. (Although fewer in number, young women also entered into apprenticeships in medieval times.) An apprenticeship was a two-way street. While the apprentice had much to learn and much to gain, a good master took great pride in imparting skill and wisdom in someone who desired to both enter into the essence of his life and then pass on to others what he learned. The master had the great responsibility and joy of training someone who wanted to be as much like him as possible.

Against this backdrop, consider Jesus' actual model of disciple making. He gathered a small band of novices around himself and simply lived with them for three years as a master of the art of living. He invited twelve novices and a few other close friends into the essence of life in the kingdom and instructed them to pass on to others what they learned. Apprenticeship to Christ—both then and now—is *not* learning "facts about" or reciting a magic phrase or the forgiveness of sins. It is the *experience* of theology. It is a methodology of transfusion, the process of allowing Jesus' thoughts, emotions, will, behavior, and relationship skills to become our own.

The intent in this section—the next four days—will be to meet the teacher and perhaps, along the way, to dismiss some false views of God as anything but a good master. I hope you'll see Jesus in a new light, with new eyes. The desire is to reveal the Master of our apprenticeship as he really is—a *community* (Day 5) of *compassion* (Day 6) and *creativity* (Day 7). We will also examine the incarnation (Day 8) as his present and experiential plan for apprenticeship. God incarnate in Christ, Christ incarnate in us.

The next four days are for learning more about the Master of living and beginning to try on some of his approaches to life.

DAY 5

Desiring to Dance with the Trinity

God as Joy in Motion

The kingdom of heaven is peace and joy in the Holy Spirit. Acquire inward peace, and thousands around you will find their salvation.

—St. Seraphim of Sarov[1]

I met with God at an Irish Pub last week. He was about six foot five and spoke with a slight southern accent. He drank sweet tea, but probably would have had a beer if it had been later in the day.

Okay, maybe Mark isn't God; but he was pretty big, and he had been working most of the items on a Supreme Being's job description. The problem was that, with all his creating and being omnipresent and stuff, he was feeling worn out— Mark, not God. But let me back up.

A few days prior, my friend had emailed me to see if we could meet. Being a psychologist who likes to listen but not charge fees, I get that a lot. We decided on a place that was on my way home from work, Paddy's Irish Pub. It is a pretty cool spot, an exact replica of a historic 1800s tavern that had been shipped over from Ireland—brick for brick and stool for stool. The owner had a U2 CD playing in the background and lots of bad food around in case you needed even more help being transported away from the rural Georgia surroundings to Ireland.

A few years after graduating, Mark gave up on his vision of being a professional baseball player—he had been an outstanding catcher for his college team—and drove over to Georgia in an old car; a few bucks and a new dream was all he brought. He wanted to build a safe haven for boys who had been abused or in need of more support than their families could offer. His motto was, "Attempt something so great for God that it is doomed to fail unless he is truly in it."

Well, God—the real one—must have been in it. Twenty years and hundreds of acres later, Mark didn't just build a home; he constructed a ranch—a whole community really—that has been called home by over 500 children. And that is why Mark reminds me of God. They are both real big guys who work tirelessly behind the scenes to make sure kids get hugged and adults get paid. They both dream huge dreams and then make them happen. And if either one ever sits down to take a break, you are sure to see children climbing all over his lap.

So I was surprised when Mark took a big swig of sweet tea and said, "Do you ever feel like life just punched you in the gut, and you wonder if you'll ever be able to stand back up?"

And before I could think up something to say that sounded smart, like "yes," or something empathetic like, "my stomach's hurting right now," he hit me with another one. "Do you ever feel like you are walking along with God, having a good time, and then he changes all the rules on you and doesn't say anything about it, until you start wondering where he is and you feel completely lost?"

Dang, I thought. And the only other thing that came to mind was what I had heard another friend and fellow psychologist say when faced with a similar dilemma: "You need professional help." So I kept my mouth shut and kept eye contact while listening to the U2 music for inspiration. Bono began singing *I Still Haven't Found What I'm Looking For,* and somewhere between "I have climbed highest mountains" and "I believe in the kingdom come," my mind started drifting. Fortunately, Mark didn't notice and kept talking.

I was daydreaming about the time I was invited to a birthday bash for a pretty famous couple. I'd tell you who they are, but that would be name dropping and both Billy Graham and Mother Teresa told me I should stop doing that and just trust that people will still like me even if I don't hang around with celebrities.

So anyway, I'm at Larry and Rachel Crabb's birthday party and they've rented this really nice country club and everyone is wearing tuxedoes and evenings gowns like it's a high school prom. There are a lot of other people there I recognize but shouldn't mention their names either, but I really was hoping to get to sit at the table with Philip Yancey because when I had more hair it looked a little like his and I thought we might be able to commiserate, but that's beside the point.

The point is, it was a wonderful evening with gourmet food and a kaleidoscope of colorful stories and images from a couple of lives that had been extremely well-lived. Everything was great until the very end. That's when the MC announced that it was time for the dancing to start. Then I really had a flashback to my high school prom, and it wasn't a pretty picture.

To say I have two left feet is an insult to left feet everywhere. It's not really my fault that I can't dance. I was brought up to believe that dancing was one of the deadly sins, along with drinking, smoking, and going to pool halls or movie theaters; so I didn't get much practice with any of that. And dancing was toward the top of the mortal sin list, just behind murder. In fact premarital sex was specifically forbidden for fear that it might lead to dancing. So, I didn't dance at the birthday party.

I still had a good time, and the next night I went to another event that was part of the celebration. We met in a large metal barn on a ranch that sat pretty high up in the Rocky Mountains. We ate barbecue, baked beans, potato salad, and corn on the cob and washed it down with unsweetened iced tea. The best part was, I didn't see a bandstand anywhere.

But before you could say "hoe down," everyone was pushing tables out of the way and forming two large squares of blue jeans and flannel. I found myself standing on the southern boundary of the inside square. And before I could excuse myself to go to the bathroom for an hour or so, the music started up, and someone who I think was an auctioneer at his day job started telling us all what to do with our hands and feet. Just as I was thinking I'd like to tell him what to do with his cowboy hat, a woman whom I'd never seen before hooks me by the arm and turns me in a complete circle before turning on a dime and leaving me for a younger man.

There was nowhere to go but back and forth and around in circles, and there was nothing to do but slap your heels and smile like you were actually enjoying it. And to tell you the truth, with someone telling you how to dance and most everyone else looking foolish too, it wasn't very long until I was enjoying it. Quite a lot actually, and after about fifteen minutes I looked down at my feet and realized they both were a couple of dancing machines, and then I lost most of my sense of separateness from the universe and got lost in the music.

When the music stopped, it is very likely I was the saddest person in the room, and maybe the only one thinking about becoming a professional square dancer.

It was at about that moment in my daydream, Mark, the tall guy in my first story, says something that sounded like it had a question mark at the end of it. So I snap back to the present moment just in time to hear him repeat the question for what I hope was the first time.

"Do you ever feel like the joy is gone, like you are just going through the motions with the weight of the world on your shoulders?"

"I do," I say, "I used to feel that way so often I was embarrassed to tell anyone."

"What's changed for you?" he asks.

"Well, it's more like 'what's changing?' I'm in process. And I don't know what changed exactly, but it seems to have a lot to do with coming to a different way of viewing God."

"What?"

"For much of my life I saw God as some combination of a shop foreman and cosmic sheriff who was more concerned with my productivity and blunders than he was with my joy and creativity."

"How do you see him now?"

"I'll only tell you if you promise you won't laugh."

"You got it," he says.

"I see God as an amazingly loving and joyful community of three persons sharing the same essence. I see God as a dancing Trinity who wants me to join in with him, uh, them."

"Join in with them?" Mark asks—laughing.

"Yes, I believe that when I am most myself I am most like the Trinity—pulsating with creativity and compassion and in step with the community of his love. And when I feel the most exhausted, well, I've usually fallen out of step with the Trinity."

"And they are dancing, the Trinity, and they want you to dance with them?"

I smile. "Yeah, and I forgot to tell you. I can dance now."

Reflection

Invitation to a Dance

I n his wonderful little book, *Experiencing the Trinity*, Darrell
Johnson reminds us that *"at the center of the universe is a
relationship; at the center of existence is a loving community.
And that it is both out of and for this relationship that you and
I were created. I have become convinced that the notion of God
as a community of love is the heart of Christian theology. Love
and intimate relationship is the language of the universe."*[2]

These thoughts are far from new. Augustine likened the Trinity
to a lover, his beloved, and the love between them. C. S. Lewis
adds harmony to this notion by asserting that the most fundamental thing about the relations in the Trinity is that they are
interactions of mutual love and delight.

Perhaps God placed the best analogy for understanding the
Trinity in nature—so that all could see. Imagine that if a couple
is deeply in love, fully known to the other, fully accepted and
adored, and if this love is being expressed through the physical
act of making love, and if there is a mutual desire to create new
life, and if at the precise instant of creation the two have become
lost in each other and waves of bliss, then that, I believe, is the
moment when it is possible to have the best appreciation for
the Trinity. The two lovers become three and the three for an
instant in time are one.

Now, if all that is too graphic, no problem, we can dial things
back down a bit. We can stop by simply envisioning the Trinity
with our original picture, as a dance—you know, the foreplay
part. That was C. S. Lewis's repeated image for explaining this
mystery.

Lewis developed the idea of *perichoresis*, or mutual indwelling, and writes that God is not a static thing but a dynamic,
pulsating activity—a life or a kind of drama. He is almost a

kind of dance. And the whole dance or drama or pattern of God's three-personal life is to be played out in each of us. Or, to put it the other way around, each one of us has got to enter that pattern. We must take our place in the dance.

So what are the implications?

The implications for you, me, and Mark are simply this. If we are created in the image of a loving community of other-centered love best described as a perpetual dance of joy, then we will only feel at home to the extent that we have joined the dance. We are to sign on as apprentices, roll out the step chart, and learn to dance to the music of self-forgetful love.

The other reason for telling you about Mark is the same impetus that inspires most sermons and books. It was really about me. That particular episode from Mark's life resonated deeply with my own story. Like him I have often found myself poured out for a "religious" cause only to end up feeling lost, alone, and distant from God, wondering if the guidelines for obtaining happiness had been changed and I had not gotten the memo. Didn't my doing nice stuff for God obligate him for a little quid pro quo? In short, Mark reminded me of me.

Mark and I continued to meet at the Irish Pub to commiserate. We began to realize that the most powerful cure for burnout is to step out from under the weight of the world and to fall in step with the dance of the Trinity. God does not want worker bees, puppets, or slaves; he wants us as his footloose friends. Those are the rules—learning to dance with God and value loving relationships over pious productivity; they have not been changed. And they are the guidelines for abundant living.

When you are not dancing with God, we concluded, it is very natural to feel alone, lost, and confused.

pprentice Activity
Re-visioning the Trinity

The most foundational aspect of becoming an apprentice is
to *be with* that person for the purpose of becoming like them.
Re-visioning God as a loving relationship of three—best described
as a joyous dance—draws us in. Part of our apprenticeship to Jesus
involves learning how to dance.

Find a quiet place and read Jesus' prayer for his disciples (John 17)
that follows his commencement address (John chapters 13–16);
then slowly re-read both John 17:3 and 17:20–23.

Joy is the crescendo point of John 17:3. In fact the only time Jesus
defines eternal life is with these words: to intimately know the
Father. Joy—the emotion of union—is a dominant theme that
surrounds Jesus. Instances include: Mary when she visited Elisabeth
(Luke 1:46–56); the angels when Jesus was born (Luke 2:13–14);
the shepherds and Magi on seeing Jesus (Luke 2:20 and Matt. 2:10);
the disciples when Jesus triumphantly entered Jerusalem (Luke
19:37–38); the disciples after the resurrection (Luke 24:41) and when
they received the Holy Spirit (Acts 2:46–47); Paul and Silas—even
while in jail at Philippi (Acts 16:25), to name only a few. In fact, Jesus
tells his disciples that the reason he came to earth was so that his
followers could have abundant life (John 10:10), and the author of
Hebrews reveals that it was for the sake of "the joy set before him"
that Jesus endured the cross (see Hebrews 12:2).

Why do you think Jesus was so focused on joy? What are the
implications for your life?

After pondering these questions, go to your bathroom mirror and
say to yourself as you stare into your reflection:

> "I am an apprentice of Jesus Christ, and I can live the rest of my
> life 'with God,' in interactive friendship, receiving help, advice from
> God, joining in the dance of the Trinity."

DAY 6

Love Is God's Money

Compassion as the Economy of the Trinity

There is nothing eternal but that which loves and can be loved.

—George MacDonald

The Chicago-based rock group Wilco wrote and perform a song, "Jesus, etc.," which has haunting lyrics. I was a little surprised to see that my iPod lists it as number one on my most-played list. I find one line from that song, "Our love is all of God's money," particularly mesmerizing. It seems such a straight, secular arrow to the heart of Christian theology.

One day while in a daydreaming state of preparation for a class I teach, "Jesus, etc." was playing in the background. As my favorite line was floating past, I recalled an encounter with a little boy in Honduras. I met him while on an evangelical mission trip. Thinking back, I'm not sure what good was accomplished through our good intentions. But I am sure the little boy I met was a true missionary.

It was a Sunday afternoon. The group of teenagers I was chaperoning was en route to perform a drama in a nearby barrio. We drove around a neighborhood where the streets had no names. They also had no pavement. We rattled along over large rocks and nature's potholes. A cloud of dust followed our van.

The "houses" were about the size of a small living room. Most were made of homemade brick or cinder block and had dirt floors. A few were piles of wood and tin. Children and flies swarmed in and out of the open doors.

The vans stopped and we piled out. A suitable stage for the drama had been found. It was a dead basketball court. Two former backboards stood at opposite ends of a dirty concrete slab. Goals were long gone. The backboards stared at each other with missing-tooth grins. Garbage outlined the court. Occasionally, a plastic wrapper became tumbleweed.

I looked down and noticed I had picked up a shadow. A little boy stood at my side, hands behind his back, a mirror of my posture. When I changed the positioning of my arms and feet, so did my shadow.

The little boy had closely cropped brown hair with a cowlick over his right temple—really more of a calf-lick. He had industrious eyes and was looking up as if to say, "How can I help?"

"*Como se llama usted?*" I asked.

"*Me llama* Christian."

The little fellow's name was Christian.

He must have assumed we could talk. So he was off, a mile a minute, an auditory blur of Spanish.

At the end of each paragraph I would use a large portion of my Spanish vocabulary to say, "*No comprendo.*"

He would smile, nod, and then run another chapter past me.

"*No comprendo*. Sorry. Burros understand more Spanish than me."

Another smile and nod.

Christian stood by my side through the first performance of the drama. He put his arm around my waist. I put my hand on his shoulder.

"Jesucristo," I said, when the "Christ" figure appeared in the drama. "*Su nombre es* Christian. *Cristo*. Christian."

He smiled even more broadly.

The drama was over. Jehudy, a minister from Costa Rica traveling with us, had begun speaking to the crowd, explaining the drama.

Christian tugged at my shirt. He said something I, of course, did not understand. Embarrassed to say "*no comprendo*" for the twentieth time, I said, "*Sí.*"

Christian's eyes began to sparkle. A broad smile spread across his face. Then he took off like an Olympic sprinter, disappearing into the chaos of his poor neighborhood.

He had been gone for several minutes. I had no idea what I had said yes to. Maybe he had asked if I would take his family to America. Maybe I had promised the hand of my daughter in marriage. One thing was certain. I surely had said yes to something big!

The drama troupe was performing again as Christian rounded the corner and raced down the side of the court. There was something in his hand. What was it? He stopped in front of me and held up a small carton of chocolate milk. I pointed to my chest.

"*Sí,*" he said, eyes still sparkling. He was giving me a special treat. His special treat. Perhaps his only special treat. There was no carton for himself.

What a jackass I had been. I assumed Christian's excitement was for something he wanted to receive. I assumed his poverty had made him needy and that he stayed close to me because he wanted something material I could provide.

But his excitement was from the joy of giving. Pure Christian joy.

It would have been easy to cry. But I was afraid he would think I hated chocolate milk. So instead I motioned for a translator to come over.

"Thank you for the milk," I said. "Your gift is very special."

Then I took off my watch and put it on his wrist.

"Your name is Christian. Every time you look to see the time, I want you to say to Jesucristo, 'Help me to keep on being as loving as you are, until the next time I look at this watch.'"

That seemed right to me. I knew that every time I would see a carton of milk I would be reminded of how much I would need the help of Christ to be as giving as his young namesake.

Reflection

God as Love

I've always found the last few words of Luke 10:27 to be incredibly challenging: "You shall love the Lord your God with all your heart, and with all your soul, and with all your strength, and with all your mind; and *your neighbor as yourself*" (NRSV, emphasis added). We are called to love our neighbor as ourselves. The obvious assumption is that the writer believes that we already love ourselves, acknowledge our own worth, and put a high value on our own lives. As a psychologist, I'm aware that some people need assistance in learning to love themselves. But the gospel writer's assumption still stands—most folks will quite naturally place a high value on their own life and well-being.

But that's the easy part. We are also called to give that same amount of love, value, and esteem to our neighbor, and to return wholehearted affection to God. Why? Why do the arrows need to flow in all three directions?

I think the answer is found at the core of God's nature. God's simplest and highest name is love. "God is love. Whoever lives in love lives in God, and God in him" (1 John 4:16). Nowhere is God defined more concisely than in this first epistle of John: "God is love."

According to Teresa of Avila, in *Way of Perfection*, God's love reveals the divine resolve to hold in personal communion all creatures capable of enjoying this communion. The primary purpose of creation is to fulfill God's wish to bestow love and teach love so that creatures can share in the blessedness of divine life. And because we are created in the image of God, our mission statement is: "To love and be loved in return."

Christian, the little boy in the story, demonstrated the core character trait of the Trinity. He was in step with the divine pattern of being—self-forgetful love and the subsequent experience of pure joy.

While our evangelical drama troupe was throwing out candy like Santa during a Christmas parade to draw a crowd, pounding sticks on concrete to focus their attention, enacting scenes of cosmic conflict between good and evil, trolling for souls with fear and guilt, Christian was being a true evangelical. He stepped into my life and shared from the heart. The key to his joyfulness and to mine and yours is the spiritual power of the Trinity, self-forgetful love.

pprentice Activity
Getting into the Flow— with Simple Acts of Kindness

According to University of Chicago psychologist Mihaly Csikszentmihalyi, people are most happy when they are "in the flow," that is, when they have forgotten about themselves and have become lost in an activity, a person, a game. They are unhappy when they lose the flow and fall back on themselves. Theologically speaking, our souls become sick when they fall out of similitude with God, and they are doctored back to health precisely when they begin to resemble the divine pattern of other-focused love.

Think of at least three people you can surprise today with a simple act of kindness or love. Then ask God to help you carry out the plan today. Notice how it feels to forget yourself and become lost in the flow.

DAY
7

Emulating the Master's Creativity

The Joy of Originality

Those who have fully taken on the character of Christ—those "children of light" in Paul's language—will in eternity be empowered by God . . . as free creative agents.

—Dallas Willard

When I was seven years old, my family moved into a large white house that had been built in the 1800s. Originally it had been a farmhouse, but over time a small college town sprouted up around it. Our family was never sure how old the house was, but one morning back before the millennium rolled over, two ninety-year-old sisters knocked on the door and asked if they could walk around in the yard where they had played as children. We asked if they remembered when the house was built, and one sister said, "Lord, no, it was already an old house when we moved in."

An old farmhouse was a fun place to grow up. There were plenty of trees to climb, a yard big enough for a softball game, a wraparound porch for skateboarding—with metal wheels at that time—and two old barns that doubled as opposing forts.

But the best features of the house were the neighbors it came with, Karl and Sarah. They were the type of people who could give Christianity a good name. Both were kind, gentle folk that tended to their own business unless you got sick or had a flat tire.

Karl was a big man who was surprisingly soft-spoken. He lived in coveralls except when heading to church. The blue denim was always coated with dust from his woodshop, where he worked as a cabinetmaker. His place of business was a dilapidated shed about thirty paces from his back door. It was covered in black tar paper like a hastily wrapped present and always appeared to be one good gust of wind from falling over. Behind the shed was a huge stack of wood, most of which had been salvaged from discard piles.

I'll never forget the first time I walked into Karl's shop. I looked around in amazement at both his marvelous wooden creations and the surprising place where they were being produced. The dirt floors were covered with several inches of wood shavings and sawdust. A coal-burning stove stood in the center of the room. Orange embers glowed out through a metal grate, reminding me of a Halloween jack-o'-lantern. Wood of all sizes and shapes leaned against three of the walls. The only large machines were a table saw for straight line cuts, a band saw for curves, and a lathe for turning out table legs. Hand tools rested on shelves or hung from the walls.

Two well-ridden sawhorses were in the shop holding up one of the most beautiful pieces of furniture I'd ever seen. It was a desk Karl had built for my father. Bookshelves that would sit on top were standing against the back wall waiting for a final coat of varnish. Soon the two pieces would be forever united in my father's study.

Over the years that followed, Karl would fill our home with his wooden creations: another desk, kitchen cabinets, bookshelves, screen doors, and custom closets—everything our old house needed for its face-lift. But our home was not the exception. I remember hearing one man tell my father that he suspected every house in town—including God's—boasted at least one of Karl's pieces of pinewood art.

Karl's most visible contribution to the community was the church steeple. Some were ready to dub it the ninth wonder of the world. For almost four decades now it's been pointing passersby toward heaven. But the wonder of it is that Karl built it without ever climbing on the roof or taking a measurement. He just showed up at the church one morning, stared at the roofline for a while, wrote something on a napkin, and went back to his shop. About a week later he pulled up with the gigantic steeple in tow. It was hoisted to the top of the church where it adhered to the roof like a Tupperware lid. Four braces, a few nails, and the work was done.

When I got a little older—but still too young to be in the same room with power tools—I asked Karl if he wanted to hire me. I could tell it really hurt him to tell me no. But as a carpenter, he knew I'd need all my fingers later in life. He didn't leave me with empty pockets, however. Even though he had recently mown his lawn, he pointed out a small patch he claimed needed a fresh cut. I walked behind his lawn mower for a while. The grass was already so short I couldn't tell where I had been. He stopped me after about fifteen minutes, bragged on my hard work, and gave me enough change (fifteen cents) to buy a 16-ounce Royal Crown Cola and a Baby Ruth candy bar big enough to grip like a baseball bat.

About ten years later, when I was old enough to do some real work and smart enough to keep my fingers away from the business part of a table saw, Karl asked me if I wanted to work with him in the shop. I turned him down. I must have reasoned that appreciating God's creation from a lifeguard stand was more advantageous than learning to create beautiful things myself. It was a poor decision.

A few decades have passed and I deeply regret the lost opportunity of becoming Karl's apprentice for a summer. Not just because my current tool collection could fit in the glove compartment of a car. I regret that I did not spend time with that gentle giant whose life bore such a striking resemblance to Jesus. I regret that I didn't pick up more of his simple approach to being with God as he worked and seeing God in the people he worked for. And I regret not having my own wood shop in the backyard or at least having the ability to plane a door, build a closet, or create a cabinet from discarded scraps of wood.

Karl may have been more like Jesus than anyone I've ever met. And I don't just mean that he was a carpenter or that his place of business looked like a stable. No. In Karl you could see the three most prominent character traits of God. He was *creative*. He could breathe new life into scraps of wood others had left for dead. He was *compassionate*. Karl was a poor man, but he would give you his last cent if you needed it. Karl was part of a loving *community*. He lived his simple life connected to his family, his friends, and his church.

Reflection
God Is Pretty Creative

Michelangelo, a fairly creative guy in his own right, once said: "In every block of marble I see a statue as plain as though it stood before me, shaped and perfect in attitude and action. I have only to hew away the rough walls that imprison the lovely apparition to reveal it to the other eyes as mine see it." He saw his David encased in marble and then chipped away what was not part of the perfect image.

Karl had a similar gift. He wasn't a wood carver. His creativity wasn't the ability to see the perfect squirrel buried in a block of wood and whittle away the rest. But he could look at a pile of warped and weathered wood scraps and envision the creation it could become.

God is pretty creative too. He formed an entire universe out of nothing. He made up space and time, monkeys and mangos, heat and cold, a vast palette of colors, and all the smells from skunk spray to cherry blossoms out of his own head—which he also invented. He thought it. He saw it and then he sang it into existence. He designed every atom in my body, yours too. And, like Michelangelo, he can see the *imago Dei*—the perfect image of himself—buried inside us and then uses life and a chisel of grace to hew away the rough walls that imprison that image so others can see it too. And like Karl, he seems particularly partial to redeeming beauty from discard piles.

To be God's apprentice, to be like him, means among other things to be our most creative selves, because he is creative. This goes a long way toward explaining why we take such spontaneous delight in all sorts of creative activities—coming up with new ways to bake cakes, string words together, turn emotions into music, do our jobs, and say "I love you." God has made us to experience joy in imitating, in a creative way, his creative activity.[1]

Apprentice Activity

Being Creative "with-God"

It is vitally important to find and give time to creative activity—whether that be expressing our emotions through modern dance or tinkering with a carburetor to produce more horsepower—and to realize that in the joy of the creativity lies a spark of divine presence within.

Make a list of everything you do that is creative. Don't leave anything off the list. Perhaps you enjoy

- sewing
- creating new skills in Little League baseball players
- arranging words on paper
- cooking from scratch
- painting
- working with wood
- scrapbooking
- solving conflicts
- dreaming up new ways to make a business work, etc.

What's your list?

_____

_____

If you have multiple items on your list, then ask yourself a question to narrow the list: "Which of these creative tasks is most life giving?" Then once you've narrowed the list to one, block out enough time to be creative "with-God" for a while today and then try to make it at least a weekly habit.

DAY 8

Tapping into the Force

Christ Incarnate in Me

When Jesus says "Man does not live by bread alone," he is referring to $e = mc^2$ and he is referring to the energy of God.

—Dallas Willard

What is the most embarrassing time of your life? Were you ever caught unprepared to give a speech? Forget the lyrics while singing a solo? Rip the seat out of your pants bending over to pick up something?

My most embarrassing moment stretched into five hours. It began with amazing generosity and the best of intentions, but it became an agonizing dark night that I thought would never end.

A new friend arranged for a very special afternoon of golf. He put together a foursome that in addition to the two of us included an old friend, John Ortberg, and an honest-to-goodness golf pro who spoke with an English accent that gave him instant credibility. We were to tee off from the Stanford University golf course, the same one the illustrious Cardinal golf team used for matches, the same one Michelle Wie was practicing on that very afternoon.

I'll need to digress for just a bit in an attempt to save what little face I have left after that day. I love sports. I've enjoyed watching and playing since I was a kid. It's almost an obsession. I begin each and every day with a slow perusal of the sports pages from the *Atlanta Journal-Constitution* and a cup of black coffee. Most mornings I don't bother with the other sections of the paper, figuring that if the world is coming to an end I'll be able to see it firsthand on my way to work. I've often considered looking for employment as a sports trivia specialist.

I especially like playing sports, although I did get a late start on my athletic career. Beginning school a year early and getting my growth spurt a year late was devastating to my high school football ambitions. But I played on the tennis team and later for the small college I attended. Three decades later I still play racquetball a couple of times a week, and tennis and basketball on a semiregular basis. Like a cat, I can't resist chasing after anything that bounces.

However, over the past few years, some of my favorite sports—like flag football—have become hazardous to my moving parts. When I finally decided to put the football down, I picked up a set of golf clubs. What a mistake.

For overly analytical perfectionists who have some endearing obsessive-compulsive features, golf is not a good sport—although punting may be the worst. I'm not referring to punting in football; I'm referring to the British idea of propelling a bulky, flat-bottom boat by pushing against the soggy river bottom with a twenty-foot-long metal pole that seems to weigh more than the boat itself. When I'm doing the pushing, the rudderless raft spins in circles and people on the bank laugh with British accents and point. I think the "punting" in American football can be traced to English punting. It means, "I give up, you try this for a while."

Anyway, attempting to play golf has been, how can I say it politely, a continuing catalyst for spiritual formation. I heard the pastor of a megachurch once say that the most effective plan for spiritual formation would be to marry a very difficult person to live with—he said it more succinctly than that. I've never tried that, but I got the point, having attempted both punting and golf.

So, it was with considerable anxiety that I approached the first tee at the Stanford course. And that was before I got out of the cart and observed that you had to hit the ball over a busy highway to reach the first fairway.

My friend who was financing the expedition hit first and drove the ball 250 yards to the center of the fairway. The golf pro used a similar flight path for his 280-yard drive. John, who is also a recent convert to golf, was my only hope for mediocrity. When I saw his golf ball fly high and straight, I swallowed hard. I teed up, muscled up, reared back, and drove the ball through a thicket and into traffic. And while the ball got picked up for jaywalking, it would be one of my better shots of the day.

I got to ride in the cart with the golf pro. I came to understand that part of the "gift" was to have a personal golf instructor for the afternoon. The need was as obvious as the skid marks on the highway. For the next five hours my whole approach to hitting golf balls was deconstructed. Before arriving red faced and humiliated to the last hole I had changed my grip (from baseball to interlocking), my stance (feet flared), my proximity to the ball (apparently I had been lining up in a different zip code than where the ball resided), the rate at which I drew back the club (4 miles an hour), the rate at which I was throwing the club at the ball (140 miles per hour), and where I was looking after I swung (instead of continuing to keep my head down, I had the habit of looking up just in time to see a terrible shot).

Before the day was over, and with all the changes I was attempting to incorporate, my three buddies had a chance to see a golf ball do some things never witnessed by human eyes. Michelle Wie got a chance to see this too.

I hit balls that shot away from the club at completely imperfect 90-degree angles. I put dents on the top, yes, the very top, of the club head of a driver. I dug divots a 200-pound groundhog would be proud to show his relatives, and the only birdie I scored fell out of a tree on the 14th hole.

I must say the golf pro was an amazingly patient man who had a gift for finding a compliment for a golf swing when a double expletive would have been in order. But after the 16th hole he had met his match and gently informed me that I was the most "right-hand dominant" golfer he had ever encountered and offered to run over my controlling appendage with our cart. I declined, but understood his frustration. Mercifully, after my quadruple bogey on the 18th, it was over.

Three days later I was back home on a driving range with a bushel basket full of golf balls. Point by point I was attempting to incorporate what the golf pro tried to teach me. First the new stance: fifty balls. Then the new grip: fifty balls. Knees flexed. Head down. Eyes locked. All was going surprisingly well until I pulled out my driver and started spraying shots into the woods. Then it hit me. My right arm. It's trying to take over. When I feel the pressure to hit the ball a long way, my right arm steps in and says: "I can do this! Just like with racquetball and tennis, I can help you. Let me do it!"

I stood over the next ball and pretended I didn't own a right arm. I said out loud—so the phantom limb would know I was serious—"From this point on I'll only need my large muscles." I drew the club back with my shoulders. I let them twist the club back and over my head until I felt the pressure in my right leg. And then I let that leg—not my right arm—begin the forward motion, which was mostly a turning of the hips and a shifting of weight. And that's when I saw it. Magic! The golf ball rocketed through the air for what seemed like a full minute. I know I had time for three "Good Lord Have Mercies!" before it landed.

Remembering that a roomful of monkeys have been known to type out a sonnet every now and then, I tried the new swing again.[1] Another miracle! I went through the rest of the balls and to my absolute astonishment the percentage of decent shots had raised from .001 to about 75 percent. I looked around. Crap! Where is Michelle Wie when you need her?

Walking back from the driving range, feeling more like Tiger Woods than at any other point in my life, I realized the spiritual significance of what had happened. My approach to so much of life has been like my approach to hitting with a driver. If the task is difficult I instinctively say somewhere inside, "I've got to use my right hand, my strength, my power, my ability to control." But what is really needed—especially when the task is difficult—is to tap into the big muscles, to tap into a source of energy that so often lies dormant, untapped. And while this seems to be the secret to driving a golf ball, I think the same principle applies to living life well—learning to let go of personal power/control and tap into the energy of God.

Reflection

Jesus Was Smarter Than Einstein

According to Dallas Willard, when Jesus says, "Man does not live by bread alone," he is referring to $e = mc^2$ and he is referring to the energy of God. If we think in terms of Einstein's equation, Jesus' words take on another layer of meaning. He is saying, "I have energy (meat) that you know not of . . . the energy of God."

We gain insight into how and why Jesus' path works and receive power beyond ourselves as we take the simple steps of a trusting apprentice, living in his kingdom. That is to say, we can learn from the mistakes we've made while relying on our own power. We can learn to take the same approach to the events of each day that I am learning to take when approaching a golf ball. Standing next to a difficult situation with a friend or spouse, co-worker or child, we say to God: "While my natural tendency is to use my own power to manage or control this situation, with your help I will not do this. Instead, from this point on I no longer need my right hand. What I need is the power of my large muscles, that is, your power and the energy of your kingdom."

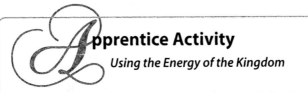

pprentice Activity
Using the Energy of the Kingdom

While it is common for Christians to be exhorted to "take Christ into the workplace" or "bring Christ into the home," this points to the deadly assumption that Christians normally leave Christ at church. Let's change that.

Ask God for guidance in bringing to mind one difficulty you are experiencing in a relationship. Perhaps it is with your spouse or a child. Perhaps a simmering conflict with a friend or co-worker comes to mind. After you have identified a relationship that is not up to par, say to God:

> "For the rest of the day—or for the next few days—I want to avoid using my right hand, my ability to control or manage the situation. Instead I want to tap into the energy of your kingdom."

Invite God to move through you as you relate to the person he brought to mind with works, energy, and power that is outside yourself.

Know Yourself

Reflections on Me—Apprentice and Student of the Mysteries

Typically in a medieval apprentice program, a young person would enter an apprenticeship at fourteen to eighteen years old and the training would last seven to ten years or more. The apprenticeship marked a decisive break from the status of child. During this time of swirling change, the young student learned not only a craft but the characteristics of the role they would eventually play as adults. If an apprentice fully embraced the apprenticeship, the result was a dramatically changed life as the student would begin to form an identity with their master, with his guilds, and with the city or residence of which they would become citizens when they completed training.[1]

Apprentices were typically from families with access to money, as the cost for entry could be very high. There were some slots, however, for those whose families could not afford the tuition. Even for a family with means, a sponsor was sometimes involved. The majority of apprentices came from the country, so for these this time of training would include their first exposure to city life.

It should be noted that not all apprentices completed the course of training. Many apprentices left service when they perceived that they could do very well for themselves by setting up trade in another city, by going to trade fairs, or even by trading abroad on their own.[2]

In Jesus' time, such an intense program of learning from a master would have been the norm. Central to life in the Jewish community was educating children in the text of the Scriptures. Usually from the ages of five to ten, good Jewish boys would sit with the rabbi and memorize Torah. The goal was to be able to recite Genesis through Deuteronomy by the age of ten. This was not called elementary school, but was known as Bet Safar. From the ages of ten to fourteen, the students would continue memorizing the Old Testament Scriptures. Besides directing the study of the Scriptures, the master, the rabbi, would also offer instruction through a process of questions and answers as tutorials.

But by the age of fourteen—note similarity to the medieval model—the best of the best would be invited to continue studying with the rabbi, learning how to apply oral and written law. And the best of these would go through even more intense training and perhaps, for a very few, be invited to become a disciple, a rabbi in training. This would require leaving everything so that the whole life could be devoted to becoming just like the rabbi. Those who did not make the cut, who didn't have what it takes to become like the rabbi, were told to "go make babies and pray that they become rabbis, and ply your trade."[3]

In his powerful teaching video, *Dust of the Rabbi*, Rob Bell provides a wonderful overview of this process of rabbi making and offers an astounding insight. When Jesus called his band of disciples, young men plying their trades, he was calling those who didn't make the cut.[4] Jesus was calling young men who had been judged unfit to be disciples of a rabbi to be his disciples, to enter into an intense three-year apprenticeship. With Jesus they would learn to live out the Torah, how to live in the kingdom. Jesus chose rejects as his apprentices.

In this section we'll take an honest and unflinching look at who we are and where we are in our apprenticeship to God. We'll examine what has worked and what has not. In addition to focusing on what we bring to the apprenticeship that is good (Day 9, the *imago Dei*), bad (Day 10, our desire for autonomy and self-rule), and ugly (Day 11, the internal tug of war between our true and false self), we'll also continue to examine why trying harder does not work (Day 12).

We will also continue to explore how a successful apprenticeship is more a matter of training *with* the Master—who knows us and loves us completely—than trying on our own to be like him.

DAY 9

The Good

I Am Better Than I Think

There are no ordinary people. You have never talked to a mere mortal.

—C. S. Lewis

I was about fifteen minutes into my *first* lecture at my *first* full-time teaching job when I encountered an awkward situation. Todd made his entrance into my crowded classroom. He was "fashionably late." Looking me over, he walked to the back of the room. I say walked, but really that's not quite accurate. Sauntered. Bebopped. Lame-horse shuffled. These would be more precise terms for his up-and-down gait.

He found a seat in the back row and leaned back in his chair. It met the back wall at a 45-degree angle. Arms folded across his chest. Oakley sunglasses wrapped to his ears. No paper, pen, or laptop in sight.

After he had endured a few minutes of the lecture, Todd raised his hand. From the look on his face, I could tell he'd heard enough. That's when I made a mistake. I acknowledged his raised hand, and unfortunately, he didn't need to go to the restroom.

"This seems like a lot of theoretical mumbo jumbo," he began. "No offense. But I need something practical, something that's going to help a kid whose parents don't care about him. A kid that's about to flunk out of school; got a knife in one pocket and drugs in the other."

Okay. That was the awkward moment.

"Well, uh, what's your name?" I stammered.

"Todd."

"Todd. You've got to understand, theory is pretty important. It's like the engine in a car. It drives everything. You want to know about the transmission—the part that turns the engine's power into useful motion. And you've obviously got a heart for that kid with the pockets," I said while trying to make out any outline of a knife in Todd's pockets.

"So hang in here, we'll get to the transmission stuff. But I'm afraid you came to class on 'engine' day."

I was smiling—toward the end. Todd smiled too. No more shots were fired.

The next two years of graduate counseling courses didn't change Todd much. He kept the sunglasses, folded-arm-approach to learning, and the swagger. He kept asking the tough questions—with less grace than a drowning hippopotamus. And, generally speaking, he kept his distance from pen and paper.

Some professors raised doubts about Todd's readiness to be a counselor, questioning his maturity. Others felt that beneath the in-your-face exterior, he had a heart that beat to help "throwaway" kids.

Todd's grades never reached the higher altitudes—you'd need paper and a pencil for that. So it came as a surprise when he declared his intention to *write* a thesis. It wasn't necessary to undertake such an ordeal to graduate from the program. Usually, that particular form of academic torture was only endured by the few students who planned to pursue PhD studies.

Nonetheless, I was flattered when Todd asked me to work with him on the project—and warned by some of the other faculty that it would be a disaster. But I couldn't resist. He wanted to develop a program to help kids who were on the verge of flunking out of school. "At-risk," the schools were calling them at the time.

He worked tirelessly to design an elaborate plan he called "Tomorrow's Thunder." Here's how it worked.

After getting all the prerequisite "theoretical mumbo jumbo" on paper, Todd proposed collecting the at-risk kids in a middle school and putting them on basketball teams. Then he would set up a detailed tournament lasting for weeks. The different teams could earn points by winning games. And they would total even more points when individual players on the team did things like show up for school, make passing grades, and avoid suspension.

It wasn't a bad idea for a practical thesis. It wasn't a bad idea for a test drive either. And that's just what Todd did when he graduated.

He went to an inner-city school system and asked for a job as a counselor. (There wasn't much competition for it.) Then he asked for the school's toughest kids, those most at risk. He got them without a fight.

How did it work? It would be an understatement to say very well. Todd's principal loved it so much he told some of his principal buddies. Soon several other schools had started identical programs for their at-risk kids—under Todd's guidance.

Soon, the throwaway counseling student became a champion to throwaway kids.

Oh, I almost forgot. After a few years of running his program, Todd was named by *Reader's Digest* as one of "America's Ten Heroes in Education."

Who would have thought that the lone troublemaker in my first class would become a sunglasses-wearing saint? Who would have thought that Todd would have been the one to find an engine to attach to the transmission he built. The engine he needed was his own heart.

Reflection

Seed of Divinity

Regardless of appearances, there is something amazing at the very center of each human being. It is more marvelous than the genetic material in a tiny acorn that can produce a massive oak tree. You and I have a seed of divinity planted inside, the *imago Dei*, or image of God.

Don't worry, I'm not about to go Oprah on you. We can never become *the same* (technically *homoousios*) as God, but we do possess the spiritual DNA to become very much like (*homoiousios*) God.[1]

In Genesis 1:26 the words of God are captured by the writer: "Let us make man in our image, in our likeness, and let them rule . . . over all the earth." The psalmist, perhaps musing over these very words, writes, "What is man that you are mindful of him, the son of man that you care for him? You made him a little lower than the heavenly beings and crowned him with glory and honor. You made him ruler over the works of your hands; you put everything under his feet" (Ps. 8:4–6).

Being created in the image of God refers to all the God-like qualities that enable human beings to reflect divine character. What are these marks of divinity? I believe the best summary consists of the five basic things we can do as humans. Like God, you and I can *think, feel, choose, act*, and *relate*. Simply put, we best reflect and represent God when we are most like him; and we are most like him when all of our components are working in harmony to produce a concerto of creativity, compassion, and community (see Days 5–7).

Often, this God-seed, or divine spark, is buried very deep and is difficult to recognize. Believe me, Todd's God-like-ness was the last thing on my mind the first time he sauntered across my classroom. But it was there. The young man I was ready to nominate for "least likely to succeed" became an image bearer of creativity and compassion, and a catalyst for life-giving community.

pprentice Activity

Seeing the Beautiful in Others— and Ourselves

On June 8, 1942, in the Church of St. Mary the Virgin in Oxford, C. S. Lewis preached his famous sermon, "The Weight of Glory." Listed below are the concluding words from this discourse. Take a few moments to slowly read these words to the pace of your slow breathing as you ponder the implications of the fact that you have never met a mere mortal, nor are you a mere mortal. Then for the next twenty-four hours allow this to change the way you interact with others and the way you view yourself.

> You have never talked to a mere mortal. Nations, cultures, arts, civilisations—these are mortal, and their life is to ours as the life of a gnat. But it is immortals whom we joke with, work with, marry, snub, and exploit—immortal horrors or everlasting splendours. This does not mean that we are to be perpetually solemn. We must play. But our merriment must be of that kind (and it is, in fact, the merriest kind) which exists between people who have, from the outset, taken each other seriously—no flippancy, no superiority, no presumption. And our charity must be a real and costly love, with deep feeling for the sins in spite of which we love the sinner—no mere tolerance, or indulgence which parodies love as flippancy parodies merriment. Next to

the Blessed Sacrament itself, your neighbour is the holiest object presented to your senses. If he is your Christian neighbour he is holy in almost the same way, for in him also Christ vere latitat—the glorifier and the glorified, Glory Himself, is truly hidden.[2]

Attempt to go through the rest of the day with this in mind. When you pass someone on the road, pause and say to yourself, this person contains the divine spark, the very image of God. When you are in conversation with someone, remind yourself that you are not speaking to a mere mortal. And when it is your turn to respond, address the person with a similar sense of respect and dignity that you would normally reserve for divinity.

DAY 10

The Bad

I Am Worse Than I Can Imagine

God should have restricted the serpent—then Adam and Eve
would've eaten it.

—Mark Twain

Not long ago I was having a conversation with my
youngest daughter who was home from college for
the weekend. My wife and I had spent the previous six months
trying to get used to parenting an empty nest. To that point
our emotions had been riding alternating waves of despair
and hallelujah. We minimized the crying times by making a
pact not to look in either daughter's bedroom until we had
the strength to turn both rooms into shrines.

So it was a great pleasure to have Jenna home and sitting
on the sofa in the den. I had been peppering her with ques-

tions about classes, dining hall food, her checkbook, and boys. Especially about boys—since I know the ways of their evil hearts.

Jenna was sitting for the interrogation with much grace. In fact, we were on such an affable roll I decided to ask a few questions about politics and religion. And it was during the religion dialogue that she dropped a bombshell.

"Now don't freak out, Dad, but I'm really letting myself question everything, you know, even religious stuff."

"That's great," I said. "What you believe has got to become *your* faith. I'm glad you are thinking things through for yourself."

I didn't say the other thought that was flopping about in my head like a wounded chicken: "Your mom and I can save you a lot of trouble. Just get a pen and I'll dictate all the right answers about God."

"I'm glad you're glad," she said, "because I'm letting myself question everything."

"Everything? Like what?" I sputtered, catching back up with the conversation.

"Well, I'm trying to look at things through other people's eyes, I mean, like how would someone born in a Hindu or a Buddhist world see things?"

"Like, how would they see Jesus?" I asked.

"Well, yes, that question is there."

"Would they, for example, see him as divine, and as God's Son?"

"Yep, even that," she said, while studying my face.

"So are you questioning the divinity of Christ?"

"Well, yeah. I'm questioning everything. I've got to figure these things out for myself."

We continued the conversation for a while longer until it was time for Jenna to drive back to school.

After she left, my thoughts and emotions began to swirl, hollowing out my insides. There was a part of me that felt proud that we had raised a daughter who felt the freedom to question, to question even what I considered to be the most sacred fact in the universe. And I felt a little proud about not "freaking out" or contacting a youth pastor to arrange an intervention. But, the truth is, I was deflated, devastated. I was also very angry, and I felt like a failure as a parent.

How could this have happened on our watch—right under our noses? Her mom and I had made a vow to raise our two daughters in a small Leave-it-to-Beaver town and in church. And our number one criterion for that church had been for there to be an active youth program. We worked hard at passing on a heritage of prayer and family devotions each night—I had even written some of the family devotion books we used. Mission trips had been as much a part of summer as sunscreen, and there were prayers before most every meal in which we called Jesus by name. How could there be any question of his divinity?

And then it hit me. Despite all the Jesus talk, Jenna had seen few, if any, examples of people who had apprenticed themselves to Jesus and experienced real alchemy of soul. Most every representative of Christ in her life had shown her more of the result of nontransformation than transformation. In her eighteen years of life she had heard sermons from a parade of pastors who were more CEOs than shepherds, witnessed a church split so ugly that Jerry Springer should have sent a camera crew, and she had been crushingly and repeatedly betrayed by a potpourri of "good Christian" friends.

My daughter had heard TV evangelists pronounce hurricanes to be God's judgment and wrath for promiscuity. She had seen the vivid horror of the World Trade Center imploding and later stared down into the crater where the towers had stood. And she had watched peers join the military and go off to fight in Iraq—in what they perceived in some measure to be a religious war between Christians and Muslims. And then, only a few months ago, she wept at the funeral of one of her best friends who died there.

But perhaps most confusing of all, she grew up in a home where both of her parents made their living from counseling, teaching, and writing about transformation, while often looking a whole lot more like creatures of dust than light. While she was still on the road back to the university, I felt like more than a jaded observer. I felt like the chief among charlatans.

Reflection

Honesty Is the Starting Block for Change

Am I being too hard on myself and other Christians? Maybe, but I am also motivated by the words of C. S. Lewis: "What we have been told is how we can be drawn into Christ—can become part of that wonderful present which the young Prince of the universe wants to offer to His Father—that present which is Himself and therefore us in Him. It is the only thing we were made for."[1]

But this is so difficult to do. Dallas Willard, America's answer to C. S. Lewis, echoes this sentiment. "What the right [conservatives] and left [liberals] have in common is that neither group lays down a coherent framework of knowledge and practical direction adequate to personal transformation toward the abundance and obedience emphasized in the New Testament, with a corresponding redemption of ordinary life. What is taught about Jesus has no natural connection to entering a life of discipleship."[2]

Harm resulting from the lack of authentic transformation is set ablaze in a story conveyed by Ron Sider. It was told to him by Graham Cyster, a Christian from South Africa.

One night, he [Graham] was smuggled into an underground Communist cell of young people fighting apartheid. "Tell us about the gospel of Jesus Christ," they asked, half hoping for an alternative to the violent communist strategy they were embracing.

Graham gave a clear, powerful presentation of the gospel, showing how personal faith in Christ wonderfully transforms persons and creates one new body of believers where there is neither Jew nor Greek, male nor female, rich nor poor, black nor white. The youth were fascinated. One seventeen-year-old exclaimed, "That is wonderful! Show me where I can see that happening." Graham's face fell as he responded that he could not think of anywhere South African Christians were truly living out the message of the gospel. "Then the whole thing is a piece of sh—" the youth angrily retorted. Within a month he left the country to join the armed struggle against apartheid—and eventually giving up his life for his beliefs.[3]

I believe that the essence of sin is the fear that God does not have our best interest at heart. The result of sin is to take matters into our own hands, to be in control, to obey ourselves, and to move away from an apprenticeship of conversation, communion, and connection to the Master. Choosing this path does not make a person worthless, but it can result in becoming lost.

But being off course is not necessarily a bad thing. If we can find the honesty to admit the utter ruin that results from living life severed from the energy of God, we can stop confusing those who may be looking to us for some glimmer of hope that it is actually possible to be transformed into an image bearer. According to Dallas Willard, "the intelligent person recognizes that his or her well-being lies in being in harmony with God and with what God is doing in the 'kingdom.'"[4]

pprentice Activity
Owning the Bad

[*Warning:* This may be painful.] Find a quiet place for reflection. Consider that apart from God's presence and grace, your soul is lost and ruined. Think about how each of the dimensions of you—thoughts, emotions, will, behavior, and relationships—functions when God is not orchestrating your life. Then bring two questions before your mind:

1) How do things go in my life when I am in control instead of God?
2) What are the ways I can make sure I am allowing God to be God—today?

DAY 11

The Ugly

Accepting My Personal Altar

Therefore, I urge you, brothers, in view of God's mercy, to offer your bodies as living sacrifices, holy and pleasing to God—this is your spiritual act of worship.

—Romans 12:1

It was a crisp autumn afternoon. The leaves were aflame as I packed and left the rustic retreat center. The last two days had been more intense than I had bargained for—patching together a multimedia-based retreat in a camp setting where the most recent advance in technology had been the flush toilet.

So to celebrate both the glorious day and my survival, I decided to take the scenic route back home. It would only add an hour and I'd still be back before dark. Two hours later

I stopped at a service station for directions. Since it was the second time I'd passed the same station—which had great pride in its boiled peanuts—I thought it was a good idea. That's when I discovered I was a full hour and part of a state farther from home than when I set out, and that I hate boiled peanuts. Thank goodness it was a beautiful day.

Finally headed in the right direction, I returned to enjoying the drive. But within a few miles I saw something that would delay my trip even more. It was a large blue and green billboard inviting me to pull over and see the "Gigantic Ten Commandments" just four miles ahead. I had been able to ignore all the "See Rock City" imperatives, but who could resist colossal commandments? Not me, especially since I was pretty sure I had broken at least one of them when I spit out the boiled peanuts and needed to check to confirm the commandment number.

Four miles later I turned off the road and drove under a white archway that read "Fields of the Woods." It was the entrance to a scenic dell between two small mountains. I continued on into the valley, parked, and climbed out of the car. I stared up in dropped-jawed amazement at a 300-foot-wide tableau that occupied most of a mini-mountain. There was no problem with truth in advertising.

The mountainside I was gawking at had been landscaped to form the shape of an open Bible. Lush green grass served as the two "pages" that held the gigantic Ten Commandments. Each Roman numeral and English letter was set in concrete font that measured about five feet high and four feet wide. Each shape was painted white and stood out from the green grass in dramatic 3-D. I learned later that "The World's Largest Ten Commandments," like the Great Wall of China, is visible from orbit. The Soviet cosmonaut Yuri Gagarin may not have seen God in space, but if he'd looked down he could have read one of his classics.

Anyway, I couldn't resist climbing the stairs that ascended through the center of the Commandments. I counted each

somewhat-high step and discovered there are 350 of them—
and that sometimes it's better not to be so compulsive. During
the climb I saw that the tablet to my left was set on top of
a foundational rectangle that read "Major Prophets" in the
same concrete letters. To my right, commandments VI–X
were constructed on top of the words "Minor Prophets." I
didn't get the connection, but continued my assault on the
giant tablets.

By the time I completed the steep climb, my legs were
burning. Besides the counting, I had distracted myself from
the pain by entertaining the notion of taking photographs of
people standing next to certain commandments. I pictured
my daughters next to number VI, and myself next to IV. I'll
keep the rest of the album to myself.

Standing breathless at the top, I saw an unpleasant sight.
There were more steps! These led in two directions which
reunited at the base of a giant open Bible called "The World's
Largest Testament." What are fifty more steps when you've
come this far? I took a few deep breaths and trudged on. Arriving at the second summit, I discovered two things. The giant
Bible was permanently opened to Mathew 22:37–40, which
contains Jesus' summary of the Ten Commandments:

> Thou shalt love the Lord thy God with all thy heart, and with
> all thy soul, and with all thy mind. This is the first and great
> commandment. And the second is like unto it, Thou shalt
> love thy neighbor as thyself. On these two commandments
> hang all the law and the prophets.
>
> KJV

The second thing I discovered was more steps. You could
continue your journey into and through the Bible by using a
staircase inside. Before completing the trip, I stepped back,
sucked in some more of the cool mountain air, and pon-
dered how much the giant Bible, when viewed from the side,
resembled a giant altar. After a few moments, I ignored the

burn, and climbed to the top of the "The World's Largest Testament."

The trek finally over, I walked out on top of the "altar," which had become an observation deck. I looked out across the valley and into the face of the adjacent mountain. I felt a little ashamed. The whole time I had been climbing, I was collecting information to support the case that this was the most ridiculous construction project since the tower of Babel. But as I looked out, my thoughts began to surprise me. Tears were now running down my cheeks and I felt an unexpected sense of being close to God, like there was something I was supposed to get from all this. Odd!

On the two supreme commandments hang all the law and the injunctions of the prophets. This Scripture was now unfurled below me like a gigantic quilt of green and white. And standing atop a ridiculously large Bible, which seemed more like an altar, I realized in some place below my brain that the only way to keep Jesus' commandments was to place oneself on an altar as a living sacrifice, crying out to God in humility and helplessness.

And that is just what I said to God. "I can't do this. I can't love the way you want me to. The only hope that I have to love like you is for you to love through me. For *me* it's over. It must be over. For *us*, I hope, we're finally beginning."

Reflection

Peaks and Valleys of Spiritual Formation

I believe there are three unparalleled mountain peaks that tower over the landscape of Scripture. Each points upward like massive steeples to the same image, altar theology. The first summit is the picture of Abraham, knife drawn, standing over his much beloved, much anticipated son. This frozen moment in faith serves as an indelible icon of radical trust. The second peak is a young teenage girl praying outside of her village. She believes she's talking to an angel. She believes that she will become pregnant out of wedlock and bear great shame. Yet she says, "May it be to me as you have said" (Luke 1:38). The third image is of her grown son, Jesus. He's going into a garden to set right what had gone so wrong in an earlier garden. Facing torture and death, sweating drops of blood, all alone, he utters the words that cause Eden's gates to swing open again: "May your will be done."

What is the Mariana Trench of Scripture, the lowest low? It occurred first in Eden, then on most every page of the Bible, and for me several times each day, even on good days. It began when Adam and Eve say without words, "I don't trust you, God. I don't believe you have my best interest at heart. My will be done." It's the choice of self-sufficiency that points downward to valleys that separate mountains. It points to grasping and hiding and separation from God.

But the responses of Abraham, Mary, and Jesus rise up like Himalayan peaks, an alternative lifestyle, the choice of willingness over willfulness. From those three altars, from that one Easter tomb, emerges the father of the three monotheistic religions, the mother of the Christ child, and the Lord of all creation, as well as Paul's injunction for all who would follow after Christ: to ascend to the holy altar and stay there as a living sacrifice.

Apprentice Activity
Living Sacrifices

Anthony A. Hoekema begins his important book, *Created in God's Image*, with the following quote:

> To be human in the truest sense, therefore, means to love God above all, to trust and obey him, to pray to him, and to thank him. Man is bound to God as a fish is bound to water. When a fish

seeks to be free from the water, it loses both its freedom and its life. When we seek to be free we become slaves to sin.[1]

Dallas Willard suggests that obedience is the engine that pulls the train of spiritual formation.

Take fifteen to twenty minutes to quiet yourself, and then slowly read through the Alpine passages of Scripture (Gen. 22:1–14; Luke 1:26–38; Matt. 26:36–42) and Paul's words in Romans 12:1. Wait a few minutes before you return to your day and ask God if there is anything he would like to share with you concerning the meaning of these passages to your life and how you live the rest of the day.

DAY 12

The Beautiful

A *"New" Vision of Me*

> The "image" means that we are God's "offspring" (Acts
> 17:28), His kin; it means that between us and Him there is a
> point of contact and similarity.
>
> —Kalistos Ware, *The Orthodox Way*

Let's review. At this point you are either eleven days into a monthlong experiential training program for becoming an apprentice to Jesus, *or* you've arrived here in a less systematic way, *or* you let the book flop open to this spot. If you are here by either of the first two paths, you know that the first section (Days 1–4) presented the need to move beyond a theology of justification alone if we actually are to become like Jesus. If you let the book fall open in search of inspiration, you've likely played way too much Bible roulette and should go back to page one.

Salvation for the early church was so much more than forgiveness of sins; it was also, and primarily, the journey toward union with God. Against this backdrop, Jesus' number one teaching theme—life in the kingdom—and Paul's number one theme—being "in Christ"—are two sides of the same coin. Life in the kingdom is participation in an interactive friendship with Jesus. This friendship, or experiential apprenticeship, is the process of learning from the Master and becoming as much like the Master as possible through experiencing the mystery of Christ within (Col. 1:26–27) and living a "with-God" life.

In the second section (Days 5–8) we "met the Master." God was described as a community of compassion and creativity, and it was suggested that we are most ourselves when we are most like him—compassionate, creative, and caught up in a community of self-forgetful love. The incarnation of Christ (Day 8) was presented along with the implication that it is also Christ's desire to be incarnate, to be "in the flesh of" you and me.

In the third section we turned our attention from Master to the novice and took a look at ourselves in terms of the good, the bad and the ugly. The *good* is the unmerited gift of being created in the image of God (*imago Dei*) with the capacity to grow in likeness to the Master. The *bad* is the fact that, just like our foreparents, we have eaten from the wrong tree and have become separate and unplugged from the source of Life. The result can be very ugly, but there is hope. It comes in the form of an *altar*, as described in the previous reading. It's the place where great beauty is revealed.

16 Blocks to a Beautiful New Vision

In the 2006 film *16 Blocks* the main characters, Jack Mosley (Bruce Willis) and Eddie Bunker (Mos Def), portray how ugly life can become—Bruce Willis's character is particularly unappealing. [*Warning*: Spoiler Alert![1]]

In the second scene of the film, police break through the door of an apartment in New York City and find two gang members shot and killed. The sergeant orders his men to call in somebody they "don't need" to keep an eye on the scene. Jack (Bruce Willis) is the one they call. When he arrives you realize this in not the Bruce Willis you are used to seeing on the silver screen. This is a "die easy" version of a disheveled, late-career cop who walks with a limp while attempting to carry both a prominent booze gut and a heavy secret into the sunset of his career. Our "hero" stumbles into the crime scene he is supposed to preserve, with no regard for protocol and every regard for finding alcohol.

Arriving at the office the next morning having "worked" through the night, Jack just wants to check in and go home—presumably to finish off his two-gallon nightcap. But instead he's asked to escort a witness to a courthouse that is sixteen blocks away. The witness (Eddie Bunker) is to testify in front of a grand jury whose term will expire in 118 minutes.

Bunker is a skinny talk-a-holic who is chatting up another prisoner when Jack arrives. The fumes from Bunker's motormouth are the last thing Jack's hangover needs. So, along the way to the courtroom Jack pulls over for more liquid sedatives. It's not long until guns are blazing, windows are shattering, and Jack is realizing this is no ordinary witness. Eddie is to testify against a dirty cop who is being protected by Jack's former partner. And there is growing suspicion that there is something very ugly in Jack's past that he's trying to drown.

I'll spare you most of the details. Suffice it to say it's not the first time in film history that two unlikely people become buddies. But what was unexpected was the path to redemption described in *16 Blocks*. Let me explain.

At one point in the film Jack has taken over a city bus— as a way of staying alive a little longer. He's made the passengers tape newspapers to the widows so the police will be afraid to shoot through the glass. The passengers are of course terrified, especially one little girl. To Jack's surprise, Eddie—the criminal Jack has declared will never change—goes over and sits down beside her. He opens a mysterious little notebook he's been carrying around the entire time. But it does not contain diagrams for robbing a bank. It's a recipe book. Eddie wants to be a baker. His dream is to open a shop that specializes in birthday cakes.

Jack's face thaws as he sees the tender side, the *imago Dei* side, of Eddie, who now is visible as a reflection of the divine image. Compassionate. Creative. Sacrificing for the community of frightened passengers. This scene is powerful in part because of the angry way Jack had emphatically told Eddie that people don't change; they were both bad guys and would always be bad guys.

Perhaps warmed by what he's witnessed, Jack comes up with a plan to release all the hostages, including Eddie. He has Eddie exchange clothes with a passenger and then let's them all off the bus. As the film continues, Jack is alone on the bus. He finds a tape recorder and dictates a message for his sister, an explanation, a last will and testament.

Meanwhile the police have discovered that Jack is the only passenger on the bus, and that they can take him out. But just before they open fire, Eddie appears from nowhere and heads back toward the bus. He's yelling, "Don't shoot!" as he crosses in front of the firing line and pounds on the side of the bus for entrance. Now a voluntary hostage, Eddie delivers the key line of the movie. He tells Jack that people can change. He references two examples, Chuck Berry and Barry White, and then says that he and Jack can change too.

And Jack does begin to change. After orchestrating an escape scene that is almost too sensational for Hollywood, Jack tells Eddie—who took a bullet to the recipe book during the escape—that he doesn't have to be the one to testify against the bad cops. Jack confesses that he was one of the bad cops and apologizes that he was willing to use Eddie by allowing him to testify and risk his life. Jack then takes Eddie's place and becomes the star witness. He tells everything the bad cops have done—including his own participation.

In the last scene of the movie we see Jack at home with his sister and some friends. He's now paid his debt to society—an abbreviated two-year jail sentence. Clean shaven and looking more like Bruce Willis, Jack is presented with a box. It's a birthday present from Eddie. Inside is a cake with the inscription "Chuck Berry, Barry White, Eddie Bunker, and Jack Mosley. Four people who changed."

The path to redemption: raw honesty about where we are, determination to do the right thing, and other-centered love. But there is an additional element for apprentices that can make change all the more beautiful. Keep reading.

We're All Lion Kings

On a recent family vacation I had the opportunity to sit with my wife and daughters in the famous church at Oxford where C. S. Lewis delivered a famous sermon which became his famous book, *The Weight of Glory*. We looked up to the raised lectern. I closed my eyes to better imagine Lewis declaring to the congregation that "there are no *ordinary* people. You have never talked to a mere mortal." The reason he could make such a bold statement is because of the theological fact that buried deep within each human is a spark of the divine, the *imago Dei*, the image of God.

Transformation is possible because this "God-seed" can grow and produce the fruit of Christ's character, the fruit of the Spirit. While Lewis stated the concept with memorable words, it was the storytellers and animators of Walt Disney that provide the most indelible image.

About two thirds of the way through *The Lion King*, Simba is hiding out in an animated wilderness with his two new friends and "Hakuna Matata"–singing philosophers, Timon and Pumbaa. Nala, Simba's childhood sweetheart and future wife, is shocked to discover that he is still alive—he's been hiding in the wilderness since long before he had a mane. She begs him to return home and assume the throne, but learns that he has changed—and not in a good way. Simba is no longer interested in being king.

Even Nala's beautiful voice and the lyrics, "Why won't he be the king I know he is, the king I see inside," are not enough to motivate Simba's transformation.

Fortunately for Simba, he soon encounters a gifted spiritual director sitting in a lotus position named Rafiki. The director tells Simba that he knows his true identity. Rafiki says, "I know who you are, you are Mufasa's boy." Rafiki says that he also knows where his father is and that he's still living. With that enticement, Rafiki leads Simba deeper into the wilderness and to the edge of a reflecting pool.

Simba looks in the pool in hopes of seeing his father and then becomes angry, proclaiming, "That's not my father. It's just my own reflection."

"Look harder," Rafiki counsels, "and you'll see."

Simba does look harder and sees his father's reflection irradiating from his own face, and then he hears his father's voice as Rafiki declares, "He lives in you."

Mufasa tells his son that he is more than he has become. He tells him, "Remember, you are my son and the one true king."

Simba then has a final session with his spiritual director, during which Rafiki wisely proclaims, "Change is good, but it is not easy."

With those words ringing in his head, Simba bolts back to assume his role as king. When Nala, Timon, and Pumbaa catch up to Rafiki and ask where Simba is, Rafiki replies, "You won't find him here, the king has gone back."

Reflection
People Can Change

I believe that *16 Blocks* and *The Lion King* are wonderful parables about transformation. From Jack and Eddie we learn that with enough raw honesty about where we are, enough desire and sacrificial love, change is possible. From Simba we learn something more. For the apprentice to Christ, change is also a matter of coming out of hiding and accepting our true identity—and that having a spiritual director can help us see this identity more clearly.

Change is not easy, but it's possible. And for all who have the *imago Dei* planted inside, which is all human beings, transformation is becoming who one already is. It is allowing ourselves to become the king who lives inside. As C. S. Lewis reminds us, we are not ordinary people. There are no mere mortals.

pprentice Activity
People Can Change

Take some time to make a list of people you know who've made a significant and positive change in the way they are living their lives and now look a whole lot more like Jesus than they used to. Perhaps you know someone who is working the steps of an addictions program, or a minister who has radically changed, or maybe you know a person who makes you feel like you are the only person on the planet when you are with them.

_____ _____ _____

_____ _____ _____

Pick one of these folks, preferably someone who lives close by, and invite them to lunch. Ask them the secret for coming to resemble Christ. Listen for themes of honesty and desire and how they allow love to flow from within. Be inspired by the notion that real change is possible. And if you can't find such a person, you're not off the hook. Your assignment is to watch *The Lion King*.

Ways of Being
with the Master

Living Life "with Jesus"

The medieval apprenticeship was a system of immersion—learning from a master of a trade or craft by being *with* that expert in most every aspect of their life. The apprenticeship was a program for formation that was intentional, experiential, and systematic. The apprentice was not learning facts about his master. He was learning how to imitate the master by *being with* the master.

When we think of Jesus as the master for the craft of life, apprenticing ourselves to him means reorganizing our lives around all the things he did and taught, but it means even more. It means learning to be with him throughout the day. An apprenticeship with God begins by being with him, living connected.

In his profound article on *discipleship* found in *The Oxford Handbook of Evangelical Theology*, Dallas Willard observes that there has been no consistent general teaching or practice on discipleship among evangelicals in the mid to late twentieth century that would be recognizable *as* discipleship as presented in Scripture or by the ancient church.[1] Being a disciple, for most modern evangelicals, has become being about soul winning, forgiveness of sins, and assurance that a person will get into heaven if he or she believes the right stuff. Ironically, these new minimum entrance requirements have produced a "nominal" form of Christianity—the very thing this later evangelical movement was reacting against— and Christians who look so much like non-Christians. As Dallas further muses, the "deficiency" produced by all this is settling for an "experience" of God instead of learning to live our lives with God.

In this section we explore a variety of ways of "being with" Jesus. We begin by observing problems that can occur when the journey of salvation becomes overly mechanical (Day 13) and does not center on developing intimacy with God (Day 14). We then turn our attention to more experiential approaches to classic ways of "being with" Jesus: Communion (Day 15), baptism (Day 16), and Scripture (Days 17 and 18) before exploring the "with-God" implications of Jesus' prayer for union (Day 19). We conclude this section by reflecting on individual differences as God's way of tricking us into community (Day 20), solitude (Day 21), and listening prayer (Day 22). Each of the next ten chapters offers a fresh look at a way of being with Jesus as his apprentice.

DAY
13

Life Is Too Long

When the Journey of Salvation Becomes Mechanical

> The whole transaction of religious conversion has been made
> mechanical. . . . Christ may be "received" without any special
> love for Him in the soul of the receiver.
>
> —A. W. Tozer

I noticed him right away. He was the only black guy in the
room.

There were about fifty of us who had gathered for an extended workshop on spiritual formation. It was a very strange
location, a commercial section of Long Beach, California. But
it seemed more like Chicago as we walked in under overcast
skies and through a stiff breeze.

The facade of our building had appeared right at home
with the other structures that surrounded it in a maze of

inexpensive block construction advertising storage space, mini-warehouses, and no-name businesses. It was a relief to be inside—partly because I had escaped the streets without being threatened by Tony Soprano, mostly because the meeting room was surprisingly warm and pleasant.

Immediately upon entering we had been herded toward our seats. En route I got a chance to inspect the gathering—a few dozen guinea pigs who had signed up for this three-day experiment in character formation, the two leaders who would be running the laboratory, and their helpers. The two "scientists" had us encircled by ten lab assistants who sat pecking away on laptops while blocking the back and side doors to anyone who wanted to escape. For the next three days the group of (mostly) strangers would be subjected to "est"-type experiences (e.g., way too much touchy-feely stuff for my taste) designed to promote "growth."[1] I was getting a little nervous.

That's when I spotted him, the black guy. He looked out of place. A flat-rimmed baseball cap sat low on his head and at a slight angle. His pants hung low exposing both the manufacturer of his underwear and the fact that these particular drawers were a size 30. I was surprised to see him in the room. While a quick panorama had revealed it was a diverse group—a balance of sexes and a wide range of ages—most of the folks looked more like me (middle-aged and white) than him. It was a pleasant surprise to see someone sporting a gangsta-like appearance to be part of the group. At least until the first exercise was announced.

After giving us a brief overview of what was to follow, one of the leaders—the one who actually looked a lot like Tony Soprano—announced that it was time for the first game. In need of both of my opposing thumbs, I didn't argue.

Tony (not his real name . . . his real name was Jimmy Hoffa) told us to walk around the room until we had the chance to look every other person in the eyes—for an uncomfortably long five to ten seconds—and then announce one of three conclusions: "I trust you." "I don't trust you." "I'm not sure if I can trust you."

With the lights dimmed and in whispering silence, we began to mingle, stare, encounter, and pronounce. Within minutes I was looking beneath the baseball cap and into the eyes of the young man with the baggy pants. I wasn't sure what words would come out of my mouth as I studied his soul through the two open windows. Then I felt it and the words leapt out. "I trust you." He returned the compliment. We shook hands.

I didn't say "I trust you" to everyone. I didn't feel it with everyone. I didn't hear "I trust you" from everyone. Each time I heard "I don't trust you," it hurt like a punch to the stomach.

The three-day encounter continued. Exercise followed exercise. Each was intended to have you experience slices of your life in concentrated bits and on steroids, to reveal how you react to a variety of people and situations. It was about insight. Why do I respond to life the way I do? What is there about me—my temperament, personality, family history, cultural experiences—that makes responding to others with the love of God easy or, most often, difficult. The "games" supplied the experiences; the leaders supplied the probing analysis—always one individual at a time and in front of the whole group, always with in-your-face reality.

At the beginning of the third day, the guy with the baseball cap and baggy pants volunteered to be in front of the room. One of the leaders stepped forward as his analyst to process with him how he had reacted to a group activity the night before.

Robert (not his real name) began. "What happened with that game last night really surprised me! When you divided us into those two groups and sent half the folks out of the room, the first thing I thought was that I wanted to be the leader. I started separating myself from everyone else so my group could see me. I wanted someone to say, 'Hey, why don't you be the leader?'"

"So what happened?"

"Well, someone"—Robert pointed to a middle-aged Asian man—"pointed to him"—he then pointed to a thirtysomething white guy who looked a bit like Fabio—"and said, 'Why don't you be our team leader. You've got the skills.'"

"How did you experience that?"

"Well," Robert went on, "my heart sank a little, and then I got mad. Who was I kidding? Nobody here would want to follow me." There was sad resignation in his voice and eyes as he pointed to his chest with both hands. "But I got past that and just wanted to help our team win."

"Robert, do you mind removing your cap," the leader said. "I want to see your eyes while you are talking."

Robert took his hat off and tossed it on the floor. His youth—he was about twenty—became more obvious, as did the emotion in his eyes.

"Go on."

"Well, I tried to hang in to help the team. But then another guy starts talking about how the game probably works and how it was mathematical and started telling us what we had to do to win."

"And . . ."

"Well, I didn't get it. It didn't make any sense. I just wanted to vote the other way, be more aggressive, and beat them before they could beat us. But I figured the guy was pretty smart and that he was probably right. So I just sat down, said nothing, and checked out."

"You're looking down, Robert," the leader said. "Sometimes that's where emotions can be found, painful emotions."

Robert had seen enough the past two days to know where this was heading. He immediately looked up toward the ceiling in an exaggerated motion, eyes wide and bulging. The room erupted with laughter at the attempt to avoid analysis. But it was too late. Robert looked back at the leader and gave full cooperation. Tony bore in for the next thirty minutes.

Fifty-two people sat mesmerized as Robert told his story, going deeper and deeper, unpeeling the onion of his life, layer after layer. You could've heard a pin drop.

We found out that just over a year ago Robert had been on the streets of Miami. He was running with a gang, doing drugs, dealing drugs, and heavily into sex and violence. But something happened. He had an encounter with God. He moved across the country and became involved with the youth group of a large church. Most every Saturday he was back on the streets, doing evangelism, preaching to crowds of young people from parking lot pulpits. It was the most amazing story I had heard since my seventh-grade teacher smuggled in a copy of *The Cross and the Switchblade* and read it to our class. But Tony wasn't satisfied. He'd noticed something tugging at the corners of Robert's eyes.

"That's a powerful story, Robert, but something doesn't seem quite right. The emotions on your face aren't matching your words. Your eyes aren't showing me joy. In fact, you seem sad, like you could cry while telling me all this 'good' stuff. I'm impressed with your story, but I'm wondering if that's why you are telling us, to impress us. I'm wondering if you are impressed with your own story."

Robert paused and looked down. When he looked back up his face had become completely still. His eyes were wide-open windows of honesty. As he began, his eyes were welling with tears.

"You know, sometimes I think that life is just too long. I mean, I want to live forever with God and all, and I sure don't want to go to hell, but sometimes I miss the way things were back on the streets. I miss my buddies. I miss the community, how we were all together, watching out for each other. You know, don't get me wrong, I'm not going back to that life. But I miss it. If it weren't for wanting eternal life so much, and wanting to stay away from hell, I'd go back to the way things were."

The analysis continued. The honesty continued. But it was all aftershocks to the bomb that had already exploded in the room. When Robert finished talking, Tony asked if anyone could relate to what Robert had said.

For the first time during our encounter, the group stood up as one and gave Robert a thunderous standing ovation. I don't think there was a dry eye in the room. Robert was our leader now, and we were about to follow him into new depths of honesty.

Reflection

The Courage to Say What Others Are Thinking

When Robert went back to his chair and sat down, the rest of the room followed his lead, except for one middle-aged white guy who remained standing and spoke for all of us.

"I just want to say to Robert, I appreciate your courage and that you were so real. And I want you to know that you aren't all alone. I feel the same way, I mean if I'm ever that honest with myself. But you made me think of something I'll never forget. Look around this room. Probably half of us are ministers. What have we done? What have we done to the excitement of community, the excitement of living life 'with God'? There's nothing wrong with the fact that you miss the community you had 'before' you became a Christian. But there's a whole lot wrong with any version of Christianity that doesn't offer you even more community and more love than you had before. I'm sorry, Robert. There are a whole lot of us who have let you down."

In John 10:10 Jesus says that while it is the intention of the thief and robber to steal, kill, and destroy, he (Jesus) came so that we can have life and have it more abundantly. This is the same Jesus who was a member of two vibrant communities—his gang of disciples and the Trinity. As referenced in the reading for Day 5, the life of Jesus reminds us that at the center of the

120

universe there is relationship; at the center of existence is a loving community.

Abundant life, membership in a loving community, constant companionship with the One who designed the universe—what have we done to take the fun out of that? You know as well as I. Somehow we've changed salvation from being an exciting journey toward union with God into a legal transaction. We've substituted the four spiritual laws for the two supreme commandments and gone from living with God as his apprentice to going through the motions of discipleship as a forgiven sinner. It's enough to make a former gangbanger homesick for the community he once had on the streets.

pprentice Activity

Let's Get Real

I have no doubt Robert loves God. But I also think he would understand what A. W. Tozer meant when he said that "the whole transaction of religious conversion has been made mechanical.... Christ may be 'received' without any special love for Him in the soul of the receiver."[2] By "special love" I believe Tozer is referring to what was missing for Robert, me, and the other fifty-one people present for the experiment in Christian character formation—an interactive and transforming friendship with God. What is missing is the sense of being part of a vibrant community with the Trinity and living as many moments of the day as possible with God and in constant conversation with him.

Take a few moments to reflect on whether or not your life feels like a reflection of the "abundant life" Jesus said he came to bring (John 10:10). If not, take a few more moments to follow Robert's lead and confess to God where the two of you are together. Do you feel as if something is missing? Do you sometimes feel that life is too long? Are you in constant conversation with the Master craftsman of life? Then quiet even your thoughts for a while and listen for God's reply.

DAY 14

Yada, Yada, Yada

Putting Talk about Salvation Back in the Bedroom

> In the purpose of God's redemptive work communication
> advances into communion and communion into union. When
> the progression is complete we can truly say, "It is no longer
> I who live, but it is Christ who lives in me" (Gal. 2:20) and
> "For me, living is Christ" (Phil. 1:21).
>
> —Dallas Willard

The TV show *Seinfeld* is on my mind as I peck these words because of some dialogue from an episode that keeps running through my head. I can be more specific. I can be very specific: it's from the 153rd episode, the 19th episode of the 8th season, the "Yada, Yada, Yada" episode.

In this installment George's girlfriend is annoyingly attached to the phrase "yada, yada, yada" as a way of getting past what to her must seem as meaningless details. George

122

is concerned that she is using this form of ellipsis to keep information from him that might be unsettling to his over-anxious sensitivities. Jerry offers the encouragement that "at least she is succinct" and that it must be like "dating the *USA Today*." But George can't let it go. Eventually Elaine steps in to offer reassurance to George, who is concerned that his girlfriend might use "yada yada" in place of something very important—like a description of sex.

George: You don't think she'd yada yada sex?

Elaine: I've yada yada'd sex.

George: Really?

Elaine: Yeah, I met this guy. We went out to dinner. I had the lobster bisque. We went back to his place. Yada, yada, yada. I never heard from him again.

Jerry: But you yada yada'd over the best part.

Elaine: No. I mentioned the bisque.

Needless to say, George was not reassured. But an old phrase was given new life. In fact, all the watercooler recitations of "yada, yada, yada" led to its inclusion in a subsequent edition of the *Oxford English Dictionary*. Check it out for yourself. You'll find the "official" meaning is

1) Indicating (usually dismissively) that further details are predictable or evident from what has preceded: "and so on," "blah, blah, blah." 2) Trivial, meaningless, or uninteresting talk or writing; chatter. In essence, "yada, yada, yada" has become verbal shorthand for a speaker doing you the favor of not boring you with the meaningless details.

This is quite disturbing, considering both Elaine and George's girlfriend used the phrase to refer to sex. But it is nothing less than mind-bogglingly ironic when you consider that the Hebrew word *yada'* refers to "knowing" another so intimately and completely that it is a Jewish idiom for sexual intercourse. We read in Genesis 4:1 that "Adam *knew* [*yada'*] Eve his wife; and she conceived and bare Cain"(KJV).

Pardon the sacrilege, but this is precisely how, I believe, much of the church has come to describe the most important personal aspect of Christianity, salvation. I think for the most part we "yada, yada" over salvation, glossing right over the intimate and transforming love affair on offer from God. And this, I believe, is why Robert misses his gang (see Day 13). And it's why Gallup, Barna, and others find so little to distinguish Christians from non-Christians. Is it possible that in our attempts to understand and control the mystery of eternal life "with God" we have placed salvation in a courtroom—juridical pardon from sin—instead of in the bedroom—intimate "knowing" of God—where it belongs?

Reflection

Created for Intimacy with God

We were created for intimacy with God, to receive his love and lavish it on others. As any mental health professional can attest, when our lives are not lubricated by love, we eventually break down, become dysfunctional.

Jesus knew the importance of living in love. He declared that living in love with God and others is of supreme importance. And at the heart of his commencement address to his closest friends (read John 14–17), he declared: "I am the vine, you are the branches. Those who abide in me and I in them bear much fruit, because apart from me you can do nothing" (John 15:5 NRSV). And at the end of this important discourse, Jesus prays over his friends and asks his Father this special request:

> I ask not only on behalf of these, but also on behalf of those who will believe in me through their word, that they may all be *one*. As you, Father, are in me and I am in you,

may they also be in us, so that the world may believe that you have sent me. The glory that you have given me I have given them, so that they may be one, as we are one, I in them and you in me, that they may become completely one, so that the world may know that you have sent me and have loved them even as you have loved me.

John 17:20–23 NRSV, emphasis added

It is important to know that these verses are toward the end of Jesus' "High Priestly" prayer over his apprentices. At the beginning of this prayer is where we find the only definition Jesus gives for "eternal life" or salvation. In John 17:3 he says: "And this is eternal life, that they may *know* [a deeply intimate, interactive, and transforming friendship built upon abiding, living in the other] you, the only true God, and Jesus Christ whom you have sent" (NRSV, emphasis added).

There is no "blah, blah, blah," here, but most ironically, given the dictionary definition, there is nothing but *"Yada'! Yada'! Yada'!"* in salvation. We enter into eternal life by "knowing" God. But for many Christians, it seems, we have a tendency to skip over the best part.

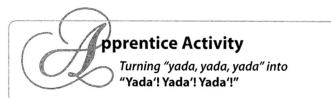

pprentice Activity

Turning "yada, yada, yada" into "Yada'! Yada'! Yada'!"

Read Jesus' commencement address to his disciples in one sitting (John 14 through 17). As you read, be sensitive to what it may mean in your life if you were to view salvation as living in intimate union with God. At the end of the address, consider how your day might change if you spend the next twenty-four hours abiding in God and then resolve to spend as many present moments of the day "with God."

[Helpful Hint: At any point you become aware of yourself thinking about either the past or the future, let those thoughts go and return to being with God in the present moment. After a few deep breaths, ask him, simply, "What should we do together right now?"]

DAY
15

Communion Ain't Supposed to Be Convenient

Being "with Jesus" in the Eucharist

All Christian power springs from communion with God and from the indwelling of divine grace.

—James H. Aughey

Recently I was confronted with a small white cardboard box with black and silver writing on top. The box was labeled "Celebration Cups." At the bottom was written, "The Convenient Way to Celebrate Communion." I picked up the brick-shaped container and peeked inside. Three prepackaged, grape-juice-filled communion cups—each with a plastic-wrapped wafer on top—stared back at me.

I was raised in a very low-church world—we never used the word "Eucharist" and instead "remembered" the last supper with Welch's grape juice and broken soda crackers once every three months. Even so I was offended by this shrink-wrapped version of mystery and had to grab hold of my unrighteous indignation. Only a sigh managed to escape as I studied this commercialized box of communion for Christians on the run.

I read the enclosed brochure with great interest and learned that through a "patented technology," it is now possible to participate in one of the most sacred traditions of church history without having to touch (or be touched by) your Christian brothers and sisters. Communion: now "virtually germ free."

That's not all. "Convenient communion" is especially helpful for the congregant on the go. "Longer work hours and single-parent families" mean fewer helpers for communion cleanup. But now cleanups are a snap. Just chug the juice and toss the plastic. And with bulk purchases, the sacred elements won't be a drain on the church budget—even if the environment will be taking a hit.

What must the Pope be thinking about this? Could anything be more profane?

I remembered a story a pastor friend had told me. His church was in the process of "remembering" the Lord's Supper. And, he confessed, he had fallen for the advertising campaign for the convenience of prepackaged elements. He had ushers distribute the plastic-wrapped cups with a wafer individually affixed on top of each. They were passing them down the aisles in silver trays allowing the people in the pews to pick and choose as they liked; it was like a reverse offering.

From his perch on the podium my friend observed that after receiving his prepackaged elements an older and crustier member of his congregation, Frank, was struggling to get the wafer un-affixed from the top of his cup of juice. His elbows had become parallel to the pew. His brow was wrinkled with determination. Frustration was evident in his squinted eyes. No luck. The wafer would not be moved.

When everyone had been served, my friend stood up to begin the reading that accompanied communion. Even as he was saying the famous words, in his mind he debated whether he should stop and ask an usher to lend a hand to the still-determined congregant. But he decided it would be best to avoid adding any new phrases to the liturgy and kept going. And just as he was reading "take this cup," Frank gave one last heroic effort that sent his juice spraying across the backs of four surprised people who had the misfortune of sitting in the wrong place. Seeing the results of his labor, Frank let go of a 90-decibel "Oh sh—!" as my friend was announcing, "This do in remembrance of me."

And that was the last time this particular congregation ever experienced a convenient communion.

Reflection

Welcoming the Inconvenient Mystery of Christ Within

My own experiences with this sacrament have become richer; they have mellowed with time. And this is probably why I had such a negative reaction to shrink-wrapped elements. What began for me as an infrequent and strangely out-of-place liturgical interruption during the free-flowing charismatic church services of my childhood evolved into the central sacrament of my Christian life as I have gained greater appreciation for both contemplative and sacramental traditions. On a weekly basis, and with the full blessing of a Jesuit priest, I am privileged to sit through Mass and appreciate the Eucharist—which literally means "thanksgiving"—as a beautiful and concrete experience of the mystery described by Paul in Colossians 1:26–27, Christ within, the hope of glory.

After a recent celebration of the Eucharist, I let my mind drift back to the first Last Supper. Jesus had sent Peter and John into Jerusalem to prepare the Passover meal. First, they had to find a place to meet. At Jesus' instruction, they followed a man with a water jar into a house. They asked not for the "upper room" but for a "guest chamber" and even possibly a humble "mud porch." While not the most oft-cited translation, I like the notion of Jesus asking for the humble "mud porch," the room where animals were brought inside and unpacked. But regardless of the translation, the owner of the home inconvenienced himself. Instead of showing them his guest room or dirty foyer, he led them to a large upper room furnished and ready.

Later, Jesus arrived with the others. At some point during the meal, he arose from the table, removed his outer garments, poured water into a basin, and washed the dirty feet of his friends—even Judas's. It was a very unsanitary and inconvenient process reserved for the lowliest of servants.

As Jesus then served his friends *the first* communion, he inconveniently took on himself the job previously held by hundreds of thousands of Passover Lambs.

Later that evening, instead of doing the convenient thing—turning in early—he delivered a commencement address to his apprentices, lavishing on them almost 25 percent of the total words in the Gospel of John. He spent his final evening with them offering comfort and intercession. And he made sure he had summarized his crucial teaching, "Remain in me, and I will remain in you" (John 15:4).

Then Jesus walked with his disciples across the Kidron Valley. With three of them, he entered the Garden of Gethsemane. Although his closest friends could not keep their eyelids apart, Jesus inconvenienced himself once more by staying awake the rest of the night—anguishing before his Father. He pleaded for "the cup" of torture to be taken away. But in the end, he chose the will of God over all other desires. He undid the wrong choice made in a similar garden several millennia before.

After Jesus' night of distress, he was betrayed, arrested, sent before "kangaroo courts," stripped, beaten, and crucified. Within eighteen hours of breaking bread with his disciples, his prophecy was fulfilled. His body had become the broken bread, his blood the healing wine. There was nothing convenient about the Last Supper. There was nothing prepackaged or germ free about the blood-filled steps that took him from there to the cross.

And although Christ's death, burial, and resurrection flung open the gates of heaven for us all, we still have to face a great inconvenience. *We* must be willing to pick up our own personal cross and choose the will of our Father over that of our own—several hundred times each day. That's tough. No, let's be honest. It's completely impossible. Our only hope is to have Jesus on our insides, alive, powerful, loving and acting through our mouths and limbs. The great sacrament is fully revealed not through the intake of bread and wine but through the outflow of the risen Christ living his life through his apprentices.

pprentice Activity
Let's Make Communion Inconvenient

During the next twenty-four hours, try to find a church where the Eucharist is being celebrated and be a participant in this sacrament.

[**Hint:** If you are not Catholic or Orthodox and cannot find a welcoming priest, you may be able to find an Anglican, Episcopal, or Lutheran church in your community that practices open communion. **Second Hint:** If neither of these options is possible, purchase suitable communion elements, download songs 10 through 14 from John Michael Talbot's *Quiet Reflections* CD, and listen reverently. When finished, read the following Scripture before serving yourself communion.]

While they were eating, Jesus took a loaf of bread, and after blessing it he broke it, gave it to his disciples, and said, "Take, eat; this is my body." Then he took a cup, and after giving thanks he gave it to them, saying, "Drink from it, all of you; for this is my blood of the covenant, which is poured out for many for the forgiveness of sins."

Matt. 26:26–28 NRSV

Following your experience of Eucharist, pray that God will be a real and living presence in every atom of your body as you go through the day. Before proceeding with any difficult task or decision, take fifteen seconds for a deep, slow breath and, as you breathe in and out, pray, "In this situation, live your life through me."

DAY 16

Baptized into a Whole New Way to Live

Some religious people might ask why I would make such a movie [*The Apostle*] and emphasize that this evangelical preacher has weaknesses. And my answer is that we either accept weaknesses in good people or we have to tear pages out of the Bible.

—Robert Duvall

Which films would you say contained the best baptism scenes ever captured on film? I'd be hard-pressed to complete a top ten list, but I know my number one. It was in *The Apostle*.

I loved *The Apostle*. I'm sure part of the attraction was due to the fact that I grew up deeply immersed in the same southern-holiness-Pentecostal-charismatic climate beautifully presented in Duvall's film. I say Duvall's film because he wrote it, directed it, financed it, sang on the sound track, and starred in the title role. I also put his name above the movie title because of his enthusiastic appreciation for this particular slice of American spirituality—and that makes me more willing to come out of the closet and identify with the religion of my childhood.

The seed that grew into the acclaimed film was planted in Duvall's soul in 1962. He was rehearsing for an off-Broadway show in which he was playing a man from Hughes, Arkansas. As part of his research, Duvall hopped on a Trailways bus and headed south of the Mason-Dixon Line and got off in Hughes. And as he recollects in an interview for *Time* magazine, "I . . . wandered into this little church in Arkansas. There was a lively preacher; the congregation was stomping and moving and feeling the spirit. I said I'd like to play one of these guys one day."[1]

Twenty-two years later he began writing the screenplay that became *The Apostle*. When all the major studios in Hollywood turned him down, he put up 5 million of his own money and produced it himself. Why? In Duvall's own words, "I hope [viewers] will be moved—moved the way I was when I happened upon that small church in Arkansas and with no warning something awakened within me that had always been there, dormant and untouched until that day. It was the greatest discovery I ever made."[2]

There are many reasons I think *The Apostle* is a great film, but I'll limit myself to two. First, Duvall gives us a character, "Sonny" Dewey, who lives in a personal, ongoing, relationship with God. Sonny actually believes the lyrics of the song sung by Johnny Cash on the sound track, "He walks with me and he talks with me and tells me I am his own." He is an apprentice to Jesus who lives his life waiting to hear an answer to some form of the question, "What should I do, God? This is Sonny. Tell me."

The second thing I love is that Duvall portrays an apprentice to Jesus who is flawed. And he presents these images in a manner that is as refreshingly honest as Scripture itself. Reading across the pages we find that almost all the members of the Holy Hall of Fame were broken. There we find Abraham, whose lack of faith caused him to father not one but two nations; Jacob the deceiver; Moses the murderer; David the murderer and adulterer; Peter the liar; and Paul the killer of Christians. Like Scripture itself, in *The Apostle* we find flaws and faith, blemishes and beams of joy. And we also find consequences and accountability.

[*Warning*: Spoiler Alert! Do not continue reading if you have not seen the film. Find a video store. I'll wait . . .]

As a result of one of Sonny's failings—his infidelity—his wife begins a relationship with a youth minister. Together they plan to steal the church. When Sonny discovers this, he turns to alcohol to ease the pain. Unfortunately he shows up at his child's Little League game while still under the influence. He encounters Horace, his wife's lover, and in an emotional fit, attacks him with a bat, which results in a coma. While this is not quite as bad as what David did to Bathsheba's husband, it's in the same ballpark.

Sonny flees Texas for his life, while asking God what to do and which way to go. Then we see it—a remarkably indelible scene that becomes the icon for both the movie posters and sound track cases. Sonny wades into a river and rebaptizes himself. He comes up from the water with hands raised and eyes fixed on heaven, symbolizing his desire for a new birth, a fresh start. Then he sets out arm-in-arm with God to accomplish as much good as possible before the parallel theme of accountability surfaces at the end of the film and results in his capture by the police, a prison term, and more good work with God in jail.

My own initial experience with water baptism was nothing like Sonny's, as dissimilar as a Chia Pet is to a Golden Retriever. To begin with, there was no river involved—at least not a real one. I was baptized in a giant, plastic, walk-in tub located above and behind the choir at our church. It sat dormant most of the year collecting dust and long-legged spiders. And it was known for its untimely leaks and the mural painted behind it by one of the congregants. It was a beautiful outdoor scene. The image was of the palm-tree-lined Jordan River as it meandered slowly in front of one of the Swiss Alps.

About once a year the pastor would announce his plans to have a baptism service. He would give us all about a month's notice which for me always became a season of intense pressure from my well-meaning father to "get baptized." Somehow I was able to hold him off for several years. I recall at least two reasons for my resistance. First, I was an early teenager—just past the age of accountability—when the issue first emerged. I felt about as drawn to the idea of having an entire congregation—which included at least three young ladies I was trying to impress—see me sopping wet as I was to the notion of inviting the entire congregation home to watch me take a bath with my suit on.

In addition, I just didn't get the symbolism. The whole thing seemed very legalistic at that time, and I had some suspicion that our church believed that if you got wet in front of everyone, it might somehow obligate God to let you into heaven, even if he didn't like you all that much. A deal's a deal and a sealed deal is binding. To say the least, the symbolism for a new birth into God's kingdom on earth was all but lost on me that Sunday afternoon when I finally gave in to the pressure and agreed to a public dunking—which as far as I could tell resulted in nothing more than me becoming a wetter version of who I already was.

Sonny's baptism and my own were about as far from each other as the east is from the west. Fortunately, I've had two extremely positive experiences with baptism in recent years.

A little more than two decades after my initial baptism, I was in the process of joining a highly liturgical church—while holding on to my original church membership as well. That's a story in itself and I'll spare you the details other than to say I didn't want anyone to be able to refuse me communion and I found a pastor and a priest who were willing to indulge my strange form of ecumenism. I figured, join them all and let God sort out the details.

Anyway, even though the priest was willing to accept my original baptism, I requested that we do it again, just in case God wasn't too keen on plastic rivers and Swiss Alps in the Holy Land. But the surroundings were not the only things changed. My heart was different. I had lived enough to know that without an ongoing apprenticeship with God, the best I could do was make myself and those closest to me miserable. I had seen the result of my sin and separation. And while I had been "born again" on multiple occasions, the "new life" had not been sustained for appreciable periods of time, nor had it reflected a genuine change of heart.

I was now longing for a much deeper change and had become desirous of participating in the symbolism of water breaking and a possibility of a new birth into God's parallel universe, his kingdom on earth, a place where his will and mine would be as one as possible. I wanted witnesses. I wanted a fresh start and to pray Sonny's prayer: "What should I do now, God? This is Gary. Tell me which way and let's go there together."

This baptism was a glorious experience. And for almost a week following, I felt like I lived on a different planet, one where my feet were at least three inches off the ground. I felt washed clean. I felt closer to God than any other time in my life. Something had happened. Something great had happened. But then, with time, slowly and insidiously I came back down to earth. I began to walk with traction, under my own power. And soon I started to head off on my own. For a long while this was extremely disappointing. I kept both the distance—from God—and the disappointment a secret for a long time. But it was precisely the pain of that disappointment that caused me to experience a second and more "lasting" positive experience with baptism.

Reflection

A *View from the Back Porch*

I have come to believe that all theology should be experiential theology and that the mystery of the sacraments should be stepped into as many times each day as possible.

When I began to reflect on my drift—I prefer this word to "backsliding"—from the warm "with-God" feelings that immediately followed my second experience of baptism, I realized that I was often distracted from the present-moment experience of God by either a pull from the past—mistakes, regret, guilt, etc.—or the future—worry, planning, or other forms of preoccupation with what needs to be done. In giving in to either call, I was immediately unavailable to the wonderful experiences I'd been having with God in the only place where such experiences are possible, the present moment.

One morning while half of the sun was still sleeping, I was sitting on our back porch. I had closed my eyes to be less distracted from the peaceful sounds of the small river that babbles behind our house on its way to the Savannah. In my imagination, I pictured myself standing in the river facing Jesus. The water was hitting us about waist level. It was a beautiful day. I asked Jesus if he would mind baptizing me. In my daydream he eagerly complied. As he held me under water, I imagined that all darkness inside, all the sin and separation, was being washed from me. It traveled downstream as he spoke: "That's gone now. It's in the past. Let go of everything that is flowing downstream. There is no need to revisit anything in the past."

I continued to stand in the river, looking into the eyes of Jesus. Then I asked him, "What about the future? How do I keep from being distracted by what I need to do, by the rest of this day, by tomorrow and the next?"

He looked upstream and I followed his gaze. Then he said, "The future is all upstream. But you don't have to swim to get to it. It's on its way right now. Just stay here with me until it arrives. When it does, we'll deal with it together."

There was a freedom in that moment that is difficult to describe. There was peace in that moment that causes me to want to re-experience it as often as possible. The primary activity of living as an apprentice to Jesus is to be with him in the river that is our life, accepting the relationship, enjoying the relationship, allowing the past to be downstream, waiting with him as the future flows into the present moment. I try to return to this image as many times a day as possible. I try to return to it so often that it becomes the day. And as I do, I feel baptized into a whole new way to live.

pprentice Activity
Being with Jesus in the River of [Your] Life

Find a quiet place where you'll not be interrupted by anything ringing for your attention. Allow yourself the luxury of focusing your breathing for a few minutes. In your imagination, step into a river and stand beside Jesus. If you are willing, envision that you are being baptized. Consider that the current is washing you clean as you are under the water. When you emerge, be in the present moment with Jesus. Remind yourself that everything downstream is in the past, and avoid allowing your mind to entertain anything from your past. Remind yourself that the future is being brought to you; you do not need to swim upstream, it will arrive in good time. Then as you remain relaxed and quiet, simply be with Jesus in the present moment without giving any thought to the past or future. Ask for nothing other than for his companionship and help in each present moment that flows your way.

DAY
17

Getting Scripture All the Way through Me

What if instead of reading the Bible, you let the Bible read you?

—Brian McLaren

I've gotten the question several times: "Do you believe the Bible is the inerrant Word of God?" Three occasions burn in my memory.

The first occurred during a job interview. It was the final stage. Several faculty members from a conservative seminary in the Midwest had me encircled, peppering me with questions, trying to see if I would fit in with the group or stand out like a Speedo in the baptistery. I don't recall my exact words, but I got the job offer, and I didn't lie.

Several years later, the administrator of a small rural hospital invited me to lunch. He had said there were a few questions he wanted to ask before recommending to the medical board that I be given staff privileges as a psychologist. I had spent a lot of time preparing for the questions. I was ready for anything he might ask about major depression, suicidal ideation, or medication compliance. I even knew his favorite college football team—Georgia Tech. But he asked only one question: "Do you read the Ryrie Bible?"

I did not. But I knew enough about that imprint for words like "inerrancy," "fundamentalism," and "dispensation" to start spinning around my head with the fear that my "wrong" answers might become targets for his attack helicopter. I swallowed hard, confessed my limited reading, and told him how I felt about the Bible. To my surprise, he invited me to join the club.

The third occasion for the question was the toughest. I was standing in front of a classroom full of eager counselors-in-training, preparing to launch into the first lecture of a course on theological issues for therapists, when the question came from the middle of the room: "Before you begin, Dr. Moon, I have one question. Do you believe the Bible is the inerrant Word of God?"

Since there seems to be no escaping the question, I might as well tell you what I said. I began with the negatives.

I don't believe the Bible is a repository of buried treasure that has been locked away through centuries of time until an Indiana Jones type of scholar could burst into its dusty catacombs and unearth the buried gems. That is, I don't think God hid key elements of "His Story" until someone armed with an IQ of 140 and the knowledge of six languages could appear on the scene and announce, "You see, appropriate parsing has finally revealed the hidden pathway." No, I believe *all* the golden rules glisten in plain view—easy to find, just difficult to follow.

I don't believe the Bible should be treated as a paper pope that can be made to speak with absolute authority on any topic simply by allowing it to flop open, spilling its guts. Nor do I believe the Bible is God's answer book on everything.

Instead, I believe the Bible is very much like Jesus with a zit. I believe Jesus is exactly who he claimed to be, God's only Son, Co-Creator of the universe, born from above, but willing to stoop low to touch the world and to save it. But I also like to imagine Jesus to be fully human. I hope that when he was a teenager his voice squeaked as it deepened and that he had at least one good-sized pimple to deal with.

Thinking of Jesus' humanity makes me feel even closer to him. This lets me know that he has felt what I feel; that he can fully empathize when I tell him about weaknesses, struggles, and temptations. Although it makes my frontal lobes hurt when I do it, I see Jesus as fully divine and fully human. And that is exactly how I see Scripture.

I believe that the Bible is the living Word, fully divine: God-breathed as stylus touched papyrus; God-breathed again as the holy words turn to pictures in my mind. Are there imperfections, linguistic zits? I hope so. As with Jesus, the marks of humanity speak to me of the trust and love of God, while only enhancing the divinity that I accept by faith and interact with through experience.

While conservatives and liberals battle for the Bible, I believe they often ignore that they are much more alike than different. Both groups tend to exegete uncomfortable passages with a pocketknife; both groups offer interpretations that would make Hermann Rorschach proud—revealing far more about themselves than about God.

As I think about the divinity and humanity of Scripture, I am challenged by the questions raised by Brian McLaren:

What if, instead of reading the Bible, you let the Bible read you? . . . What would happen if we approached the text less aggressively but even more energetically and passionately? I wonder what would happen if we honestly listened to the story and put ourselves under its spell . . . not using it to get all our questions about God answered but instead trusting God to use it to pose questions to us about us. What would happen if we trusted ourselves to it—the way a boy

142

opens his heart to a girl, the way a patient trusts herself to an oncologist?[1]

Reflection

Slowing Down to Improve Digestion

I think I'm finally getting this notion of letting Scripture read me, instead of the other way around. There was someone who helped me with this, although he never knew it. Growing up, I heard anecdotes about a distant relative who seemed to be a strange bird. No, that's not quite right. An ostrich is a strange bird; this fellow seemed to my five-year-old ears to be something more akin to the duck-billed platypus.

Hal—not his real name as I have living relatives to consider—only had three fingers on his left hand. There should have been four. He lost one legitimately while working with his skilsaw. The second finger was lost while showing a friend how he lost the first. After that he let his wife tell folks about the accident(s).

Hal was known for reading the Bible. Before he retired and back when he had all ten fingers, he was known for flipping through the well-worn pages of his Bible really fast so he'd be the first in the congregation to locate the sermon text. As soon as the preacher would say, "I'll be speaking from John 1:1–10," there would be a quick rustling of pages. Hal was off like a hummingbird on crack! And before the preacher could read, "In the beginning was the Word," Hal would have his right index finger on the spot.

When Hal retired he decided to become more serious and systematic with his Bible reading. He bought one of those "Read-the-Bible-in-a-Year" Bibles, and he did just that. And apparently he really enjoyed it because on New Year's Eve the following year he determined to read all the way through the Bible in a month. And he did.

Apparently Hal liked that as well, because he resolved to read the Bible through once per month for every month of that new year. And he did.

From all his Bible reading, Hal thought he had figured out that God seemed to be partial to some numbers more than others. The numbers 3, 7, 12, 40, and 144 seemed particularly important to God, and this gave Hal an idea. He determined that he would continue reading the Bible through once each month until he had read from cover to cover 144 times. And he did!

When Hal died, he was known for being one of the meanest, angriest, and most hateful people you could ever meet. Hal made a mistake. He got all the way through the Bible many times, but he never got certain key passages all the way through himself.

pprenticeship Activity

Getting Some of the Bible All the Way through Me

Set aside 15 to 20 minutes today to slowly and meditatively read Colossians 3:1–17, the marvelous passage about the new life in Christ. Then take another block of time to memorize the first three verses (Col. 3:1–3; we'll be using the NRSV). We'll add one verse each day to memorize as we continue the apprenticeship. If you are intimidated by this much memorization, no worries—just slowly reread the verses already covered and read the added verse a few times, meditatively. Perhaps you'll "accidentally" memorize the passage, but you'll certainly be giving it time to read you. If you need further motivation, it may help to know that Dallas Willard believes that no New Testament text is better for learning how to live like Jesus than this one is.[2]

Simmering in Colossians 3:1–17. Through the remainder of the book, we'll look at a portion of this passage each day. You'll find the complete passage in the appendix.

Let's begin by meditatively pondering verses 1–3:

> So if you have been raised with Christ, seek the things that are above, where Christ is, seated at the right hand of God. Set your minds on things that are above, not on things that are on earth, for you have died, and your life is hidden with Christ in God.

HELP IN CREATING AN E-RULE OF LIFE

To use Microsoft Outlook for creating an a E-Rule of Life Prompt for this exercise, please follow these steps:

1. To be reminded of my Scripture Plan two times per day (see appendix table 7):

    Step 1: Create a New Task Item by clicking New, then Task.

    Step 2: Put the Scripture into the task or add a link to the Scripture at bible gateway.com. Change the status to In Progress. Click the Recurrence button and click Daily. Finally, set the reminder to the time appropriate, first thing in the morning.

ADDITIONALLY: You can create an additional prompt at lunchtime in the same way simply by setting the reminder time to noon.

DAY 18

A "With-God" Approach to Scripture

Think of the millions of people who say, sincerely, that the Bible is the guide to life, but who still starve to death in the presence of its spiritual feast.

—Richard J. Foster

I'm not a fan of church signs. And where I live—the rural south—it's difficult to drive to the grocery store without being smacked down by one of those pun-laden marquees. If you are not from around here, bear with me. I don't know if the purpose of all this plastic-lettered gospel graffiti is to cause regular congregants to chuckle or to attract potential converts to a smart aleck "god" with a quip and whip. Maybe the creators are simply attempting to apply the misguided principle—that words alone can cure—to an attention-deficit generation. Flash soul therapy.

I'm not saying some of these signs aren't funny. I too have often wondered, "Why didn't Noah swat those two mosquitoes?" And when I saw a church sign that asked, "Who's Your Daddy?" I laughed out loud.

I've even seen a few poignant messages. "Want to get the last word? Apologize" comes to mind, as well as my all-time favorite. The modest sign in front of an even more modest clapboard building simply read "Welcome".

But from what I've seen, most church signs seem to fall into one of three categories:

1. Cheesy: "Forbidden fruit creates many jams" and "Doing good turns will never make you dizzy";
2. Controlling by fear or guilt: "Eternity: Smoking or Non-smoking"; "I don't know why people change churches so often. What difference does it make which one you are staying away from?"; "Please return the laptop!"; and
3. That broad, grandiose category where the lines between the human composer and God seem to blur: "God loves you and he approves this message," "If you think it's hot here, just keep using my name in vain—God," and "Don't make me come down there—God."

It's that last category that really tilts my halo. Is there anything more profane than putting our anger and judgmental thoughts into the mouth of God? It begs the question, if God really is love, why wouldn't we all want him to come down here and hang out for a few decades?

So against this backdrop you may find the positive reaction I had to a church sign a while back to be a little shocking. I was driving across the mountains of North Georgia, lost and already late for a faculty retreat. I had been racing up and down the beautiful landscape, hardly noticing the unfurled tranquility, or the road signs. My mind was in high gear, alternately reviewing "must do" lists for a half-dozen projects and grieving about a difficult season at home. Both of my college-age daughters were struggling with issues of life, relationship, and faith. My wife was caught up in her own busyness of work and worry about the significant and mounting health issues her parents were experiencing. It had been months since life was fun and unhurried. Life was off course.

And then, there it was. A church sign! I braced myself to be homicidally annoyed as the letters came into focus underneath the picture of a very Caucasian and close-cropped Jesus. The letters formed: "Come unto me all you who are weary and heavy laden and I'll give you rest."

To my absolute surprise, an immediate gush of hope burst up from within. Those were Jesus' words! The Creator of the universe and the largest religion on the planet said that it is possible to lay our burdens down, to slow down and find rest in him, to live an unhurried life. He believes that is really possible.

As the church sign grew smaller in the rearview mirror, I began to sense Christ echoing those same words to me. Was it Jesus I heard whispering through my thoughts? "Gary, it's true. Come to me. Let me take the weight from your shoulders. Trust me. I'm with you and for you. My yoke actually is easy; just fall back in step with me. Life with me can be truly abundant. Slow down and trust me more than you trust yourself."

Tears came to my eyes. I picked up my cell phone and called my wife. Her immediate response was optimism mixed with relief. That simple black-lettered reminder of what Jesus had promised—rest, relief, freedom from the weight of life—had gotten to us both. If God once spoke through a donkey, I mused as we talked, I guess it's possible for him to use the plastic letters on a church sign.

Reflection

The Immanuel Principle

As Richard J. Foster reminds us in his introduction to *The Renovaré Spiritual Formation Bible*, "The average 'Bible consumer,' publishing research tells us, owns nine Bibles and is looking for more." He then muses that this begs the question of whether we have really "achieved a grasp of the Bible that is adequate to our needs."[1] Probably not, if we are going to the Bible for knowledge alone—especially if we are looking for information to help us win a debate or argument, or if we are flipping pages searching for answers for a specific need (e.g., what does the Bible have to say about help with my hyperactive child, or acne?).

Of course, this is not to say that obtaining biblical literacy is a bad thing, nor is the point that the Bible does not offer help with specific problems. It is to say, however, that either objective can take us away from the central point. In the words of Foster:

> The Bible is all about human life "with God." It is about how God has made this "with-God" life possible and will bring it to pass. In fact, the name Immanuel, meaning "God with us," is the title given to the one and only Redeemer, because it refers to God's everlasting intent for human life—namely, that we should be in every aspect a dwelling place of God. *Indeed, the unity of the Bible is discovered in the development of life "with-God" as a reality on earth, centered in the person of Jesus.* We might call this the *Immanuel Principle* of life.[2]

Church signs can be a caricature of the two ways of using the Bible that miss the point—an attempt to flash information about or wisdom from God. And, of course, God can use even a misguided approach to his book. I'm living proof that on at least one crisp fall morning of my life, he did just that. But even in that moment, a higher view of Scripture was at work. I was reminded of the *Immanuel Principle* of life as it spoke to me from the passenger seat, calling me to slow down and trust that God is with me, always.

pprentice Activity

Meditation on the "With-God" Bible

The Renovaré Spiritual Formation Bible is an excellent resource. Edited by Richard J. Foster, Gayle Beebe, Lynda L. Graybeal, Thomas C. Oden, and Dallas Willard, it is designed to provide a better understanding of the relevance of Scripture for practical living. The editors and writers are intentional about making Scripture more useful to the process of spiritual transformation. Primarily this is accomplished by (1) identifying the major theme that permeates the whole of Scripture—the *Immanuel Principle*, or the "with-God life"— and providing essays and notes about how this worked in the lives of the people of God found in the Bible; (2) identifying the practice of spiritual disciplines in Scripture; and (3) offering reflection questions and spiritual exercises based on those spiritual disciplines. Perhaps the most striking feature of this massive work is the observation that the entirety of Scripture can be grouped— sequentially—as fifteen different ways God is "with" and active in the life of his people.

Take a few minutes to slowly read through the table below that presents a "brief overview of the 'with-God' life." Consider the implications for your life if the overarching theme of Scripture has to do with transformation made possible through learning to live a "with-God" life. Then resolve to spend as many moments of this day as you can in dialogue with God.

[**Hint:** If your watch has an alarm, set it to give you a gentle beep each hour as a reminder to stop and ask yourself the question: Have I lived this past hour with God?]

Brief Overview of the With-God Life*

Stage of Formation	Scriptures	God's Action	Human Reaction
I. The People of God in Individual Communion	*Genesis 1–11*	Creates, instructs, stewards a good creation, banishes, destroys, restores	Disobey, rebel, sacrifice, murder, repent, obey

Stage of Formation	Scriptures	God's Action	Human Reaction
II. The People of God Become a Family	Genesis 12–50	Gives promise and establishes Abrahamic covenant, makes a great people	Faith, wrestle with God, persevere
III. The People of God in Exodus	Exodus, Leviticus, Numbers, Deuteronomy	Extends mercy, grace, and deliverance from exile; delivers the Mosaic Covenant/Law	Obey and disobey, develop a distinctive form of ritual
IV. The People of God in the Promised Land	Joshua, Judges, Ruth, 1 Samuel 1–12	Establishes a theocracy, bequeaths the Promised Land	Inhabit the Promised Land, accept judges as mediators
V. The People of God as a Nation	1 Samuel 13–31 & 2 Samuel, 1 & 2 Kings, 1 & 2 Chronicles, 1 Esdras 1	Permits the monarchy, exalts good kings, uses secular nations for blessing	Embrace the monarchy
VI. The People of God in Travail	Job, Psalms (of lament), Ecclesiastes, Lamentations, Tobit	Permits tribulation, allows suffering to strengthen faith	Complain yet remain faithful
VII. The People of God in Prayer and Worship	Psalms (of praise), Psalm 150	Establishes liturgical worship	Praise, prayer
VIII. The People of God in Daily Life	Proverbs, Song of Solomon, Wisdom of Solomon, Sirach (Wisdom of Sirach, or Ecclesiasticus)	Gives precepts for living in community	Teachable, learning, treasure beautiful words and artistic expression
IX. The People of God in Rebellion	1 Kings 12–2 Kings 25:10; 2 Chronicles 10–36:19; Isaiah; Jeremiah 1–36; Hosea; Joel; Amos; Jonah; Micah; Nahum; Habakkuk; Zephaniah; Judith; Prayer of Manasseh	Proclaims prophetic judgment and redemption, reveals his rule over all nations, promises Immanuel, uses secular nations to bring judgment	Disbelieve and reject, believe false prophets, a faithful remnant emerges

Stage of Formation	Scriptures	God's Action	Human Reaction
X. The People of God in Exile	*1 Kings 25:11–30; 2 Chronicles 36:20–23; Jeremiah 37–52; Lamentations; Ezekiel; Daniel; Obadiah; Haggai; Baruch; Letter of Jeremiah; Additions to the Book of Daniel*	Judges yet remains faithful to covenant promises	Mourn, survive, long for Jerusalem, stand for God without institutions
XI. The People of God in Restoration	*Ezra; Nehemiah; Esther; Daniel; Haggai; Zechariah; Malachi; Tobit; additions to Esther; 1 Esdras 2–9; 2 Esdras; 1, 2, 3 & 4 Maccabees; Additions to the Book of Daniel*	Regathers and redeems, restructures social life	Return, obey, rebuild, worship, pursue Messianic figure, compile Septuagint
XII. The People of God with Immanuel	*Matthew, Mark, Luke, John*	Sends the Son and acts with the Son	Hear and follow; resist and reject
XIII. The People of God in Mission	*Acts*	Sends the Holy Spirit and creates the church	Believe and proclaim; disbelieve and persecute
XIV. The People of God in Community	*Romans; 1 & 2 Corinthians; Galatians; Ephesians; Philippians; Colossians; 1 & 2 Thessalonians; 1 & 2 Timothy; Titus; Philemon; Hebrews; James; 1 & 2 Peter; 1, 2 & 3 John; Jude*	Builds, nurtures, and mobilizes the church	Become disciples of Jesus Christ and make disciples to the ends of the earth
XV. The People of God into Eternity	*Revelation*	Reveals infinite progress toward infinite good	Worship and praise, creativity that magnifies God

*Books are placed into categories by content, not by date of composition or type of literature.

Simmering in Colossians 3:1–17 Continued. Please slowly reread verses 1–3 and then meditatively ponder verse 4:

> When Christ who is your life is revealed, then you also will be revealed with him in glory.

DAY 19

Celebration at Fat Matt's

Becoming Lost in Union

To play the blues, boy, you know you have to live 'em.
You've got to pay your dues, boy. You know you've got to
give 'em.

—Harry Chapin, lyrics to *Bluesman*

There is a semi-famous dive in Atlanta called "Fat Matt's
Rib Shack." I say semi-famous because we have friends
in Switzerland who have read about it online, but most likely
you've never heard of the place. But for those who live in Atlanta and like to listen to blues while getting messy with pork
ribs—and this includes everyone except for a small cluster of
vegans in Five Points and two families that Polka together—
Fat Matt's is known as the number one place for ribs and the

153

number two place to hear the blues in the dogwood city. Add those numbers and it equals standing room only.

If you are out looking for Fat Matt's on Piedmont Avenue, be careful or you'll drive right past. It's a tiny hole in the wall easily lost in the forest of fast-food signs. An outdoor row of bright-yellow picnic tables that outline the front of the building will help you spot it. Once inside you'll find a long line of folks waiting to place orders and pay with cash; but good luck finding an empty seat.

While standing around waiting for someone to leave, you'll have plenty of time to soak in the ambiance. A floor-to-ceiling glass window runs the length of the small rectangular room. It's brightly painted with images of barbecued pork, chicken, corn, and baked beans. Mercifully, there are no pictures of smiling pigs advertising for you to eat one of their friends. In contrast to these bright images, the back wall is a black and grey mural that brings to mind Mount Rushmore. The busts of four of the forefathers of the blues—Muddy Waters, B. B. King, Rob Johnson, and Albert King—emerge from a mountainside and keep a careful watch on the bands that play on a small stage in front of their gazes.

Just to the audience's right—and band's left—are two doors marked "Dukes" and "Dutches." I'd been going to Fat Matt's for years and thought nothing of the restroom doors until a friend visiting from Wales wondered aloud if you had to provide proof of being from Holland to walk through the "Dutches" door. I laughed but had to Google the word on a cell phone before getting the humor. "Duchess" has no "t." As a poor speller myself, the extra consonant made me like Fat Matt all the more.

Regardless, the room is so small that if you need to visit either royal facility during a set, the bass player will have to lift the neck of his guitar high in the air so you can pass under and squeeze through the appropriate door. And if you happen to exit as the band is finishing a song, you'll find yourself onstage with the group. The thunderous applause at that point has been quite confusing to me on more than one occasion.

I recently visited Fat Matt's with a good friend, Jay Uomoto. Jay is a huge blues fan, not to mention the godfather to my oldest daughter. He is also a talented musician who loves to take breaks from his day job as a neuropsychologist to play in a rock and blues band in various parts of the country. I think he does it just so he can see the surprised faces in the crowd when they see a Japanese neuropsychologist bending both his guitar strings and face to the blues riffs of T-Bone Walker and Chuck Berry.

Anyway, Jay and I were at Fat Matt's to listen to blues, catch up, and discuss theodicy—he was in Atlanta to teach a course on theodicy, and the drive between blues lyrics and that discipline is a short one. It was his first visit to Fat Matt's and I was hoping the music—which can be hit or miss on a weekday night—would be good.

The first band took the stage. When I saw them, my hope soared: each member of the group looked the part of a seasoned blues musician. But after a couple of songs it was clear we would not be scrunching our faces to the blues that night. They were terrible. Jay leaned over after a while and said, "This is a garage band." Not being in the know I wasn't sure what that meant, but I assumed it was a semi-kind way to say "Why did we pay money for what you don't want to hear coming from your neighbor's garage?"

By the time the second group hit the stage we were completely jaded. As they were plugging in, tuning up, and making small talk with the crowd, Jay and I began games of "what's his day job?" and "how bad can they be?" Yes, we felt guilty, but we couldn't stop ourselves. Once we started it was like eating Lay's potato chips.

There was a hollow-body guitar player from Finland with close-cropped hair and a strange style of strum-picking. He would have looked more comfortable behind a fast-food counter than on that stage. We had the lead singer pegged as a used car salesman. He was wearing sun glasses at 11 p.m. and looked a lot like Dan Aykroyd. The bass player, with black and bruised knuckles, had likely been under the hood of a car just a few hours before, and we were guessing the drummer also sold used cars—probably on the same lot with the lead singer. We decided to give them one song before heading out.

Twelve songs later we were on our feet encouraging them to play through the break they had announced. These four individuals were a blues band. We loved them. The audience loved them. Far from being four individuals competing with each other for attention, they were lost in the unity of the music, lost in letting the lyrics become stories about the lives they had lived.

Reflection

Blues Lessons

About two weeks ago I found myself back at Fat Matt's with a couple of out-of-town friends. I feel an obligation to initiate as many people as possible to the only two things in the world that go together better than peanut butter and chocolate. The band took the stage. There was an obvious leader—a fiftysomething lead guitarist and lead singer who introduced himself as "Chicago Joe." The drummer and bass player also looked like seasoned blues musicians. Then there was a kid who looked to be all of sixteen. His peach-fuzz-covered white face made him stand out from the others like a poodle puppy at a bulldog convention. But when the band played, he didn't stand out, and that was a good thing, an amazing thing, given the company he was keeping. He was pretty good.

After a few songs someone from the audience yelled out a song he wanted to hear—"Little Wing." Chicago Joe smiled at him and said, "Awe, I've played that song so many times I might not do it justice. But I'll let my young apprentice play one you might like."

And under the watchful eye of the master, that's exactly what the kid did. With a nod from Joe, the boy took a step forward and assumed the lead. Joe took a step back and sat on a stool where he began to play rhythm and harmonize with the higher-pitched voice. The kid wasn't perfect. He would have seemed more natural playing guitar in front of a church youth group. His range was limited and his voice strained under the load of the high notes. His eyes needed to keep watch on his fingers at times, and he was singing lyrics beyond what he had lived. But the kid was very good. No one seemed to mind the limitations. As a cloud of witnesses looked down from the wall, the young apprentice was learning from a master, Chicago Joe, who was playing background and smiling his approval.

From my last two trips to Fat Matt's, I've learned a couple of valuable lessons. Music can be a powerful way to experience the spiritual truth that in community life, calling attention to oneself can produce cacophony, but becoming lost in unity with others and with something bigger than ourselves can produce a joyous celebration—even when the lyrics are earthy and real. Especially when the lyrics are earthy and real.

What's the second lesson? It's pretty cool when the Master trusts us to take the lead and then steps back to harmonize and smile as we play life under his watchful eye, learning to become lost in creativity and union.

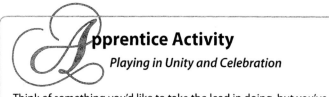

Apprentice Activity
Playing in Unity and Celebration

Think of something you'd like to take the lead in doing, but you've been putting it off for fear that it might not turn out right. Let it be something that you know would involve a movement toward unity and away from self-absorption. Maybe you've wanted to write a letter of reconciliation to an estranged friend. Perhaps you want to own the responsibility for a long-simmering dispute with a neighbor, or be the first to say I'm sorry to your spouse or a child. Whatever you come up with, take center stage and trust your Mentor to help you with the hard parts.

[**Hint:** If you need some reflection time, first think of any songs that are somehow spiritually meaningful to you. If so, listen to one or two of them and remember God's love for you. Then ask him to help you come up with a project that will move you toward unity with another.]

Simmering in Colossians 3:1–17 Continued. Please slowly reread verses 1–4 and then meditatively ponder verse 5:

Put to death, therefore, whatever in you is earthly: fornication, impurity, passion, evil desire, and greed (which is idolatry).

DAY
20

Meditation and Monk Fights

Learning to Celebrate Our Differences

For just as the body is one and has many members, and all
the members of the body, though many, are one body, so
it is with Christ. . . . Now you are the body of Christ and
individually members of it.

—St. Paul[1]

For a quarter of a century I've been making semi-regular
trips to a spiritual oasis known as the Monastery of the
Holy Spirit, in Conyers, Georgia. Almost every time I turn off
Highway 212 and drive onto the property, I begin to experience the glorious sense of a slow descent into a whole new
way to exist—far removed from email and cell phones.

To get from the front gate to the monastery, I pass over
a long, narrow drive that is outlined by two rows of mag-
nolia trees. Occasionally I'll meet a monk wearing a black

and white robe, lost in prayer, fingering a rosary. He never looks up as he walks in the grass between the asphalt and a column of trees. As the monastery comes into view, I make a sharp left and follow the narrow road to the retreat house, a three-story white structure that sits adjacent to the chapel and overlooks a small lake.

Inside I'll find my key in an envelope marked with my name. The number on the room key tells me where to put my luggage, and whether or not I was fortunate enough to get a room with a private bath. After putting my things away—never anything that will require ironing or a tie—I move on to the next movement in my liturgy. I quietly slip into the sanctuary, hoping I'm not wearing my shoes that squeak, and I begin to inhale the smell of candles and the blessed silence. I close my eyes and celebrate the luxury of thinking about nothing but my breathing. And very often I become keenly aware of God's presence as an ocean of love.

Later I will walk the grounds. This always involves a stroll to the shore of the lake—careful not to let the goose droppings soil my serenity—and several trips along the tree-lined entrance. When I need a distraction from all the introspection, I visit the bookstore and chat with whichever monk is running the place that day. It seems to be a much appreciated outlet for the few extroverted brothers.

Most of my visits include a session with a spiritual director. I'll talk; he'll listen. He'll pay attention to all my words, but will seem particularly interested when my focus shifts to how and when I'm experiencing God. I'll want him to be less like Carl Rogers—more directive—but his gentleness and lack of straightforward advice will remind me of how hard it is for me simply to trust God and live without a script. The time will end when it ends. Sometimes ten minutes, sometimes more than an hour. Always the director seems confident God will finish what he has begun in my life. I love this monastery.

If you've read Thomas Merton's autobiography, *The Seven Storey Mountain*, you may recall his passing reference to this special place. He describes the day—it was the feast of St. Joseph, March 19, 1944—when twenty of his Trappist brothers left Our Lady of Gethsemane in rural Kentucky to travel south and plant a sister monastery in the Catholic desert of rural Georgia. On St. Benedict's Day, March 21, 1944, the group arrived and founded the Monastery of the Holy Spirit. They were bringing to Georgia a tradition begun over 1500 years earlier, when their patron, St. Benedict of Nursia, "abandoned the excesses of life in the late fifth century Rome and withdrew to the desert to seek God alone."[2]

I'm one of many who are very grateful for the fruits of that historic trip. So, with my appreciation for the ideals of monastic life in general, and this plot of sacred ground in particular, you can imagine how shocked I was when a monk fight broke out during a recent retreat. I'd better explain.

A while back I was invited by the abbot—a wonderful man who looked very much like Santa Claus—to attend a three-day retreat on centering prayer at the monastery. It would be taught by the abbot, who was also the author of several books on the subject. I gave him an enthusiastic yes and cleared my calendar.

The time for the retreat arrived and I found myself sitting in a large circle of about twenty or so. To my surprise the majority of the people in the group were monks from the monastery. I could tell that because they were wearing their black and white work clothes. I was one of only four or five civilians present.

I felt like I was in heaven. For the next three days I'd be listening to mini-lectures on centering prayer from a master and then contemplating with a bunch of professionals. If you are an extreme introvert with mystical leanings, it doesn't get any better. But it did get worse.

For the first day and a half, all went well. Most of the time was spent seated in straight-backed chairs, eyes closed, and hands on laps, engaged in centering prayer exercises. If you consult Wikipedia, you'll find that *centering prayer* is a form of contemplative prayer that places a lot of emphasis on silence—of both your outer and inner world. Its roots, as is the case with the monastery where we sat, can be traced back to Benedictine spirituality. Its fruit is a way of being with God and more sensitive to his love and presence.

About the middle of the second day, I began to notice a hint of tension in the room. It bubbled up slowly but came to a rolling boil before nightfall. One of the younger monks began to express an opinion that differed from that of the leader. The leader could not have been more open and gentle in responding, but the heat had been turned up to stay.

At one level it was nothing more than a simple difference of opinion. The young monk and with time about half the room were of the opinion that centering prayer was enhanced by the use of thoughts and images. However, it was the experience of the other half of our group that centering prayer is most deep and meaningful when one continues on beyond the realm of thoughts and images and is simply with God. Thoughts and words, for this group, would limit both God, who cannot be fully captured by thoughts and images, and our experience of God.

For the next thirty-six hours tension and division in the room grew. It wasn't like the shoot-out at the OK Corral. No six-shooters appeared from under the habits. No physical blows were struck. But it did become something like a Miller Lite commercial. Instead of chants of "Less Filling" vs. "Tastes Great," it was "With Images" vs. "No images."

By the end of the three days, there were no injuries to report. Cooler prayer-heads prevailed. But for me, what began as an intense experience of being with God, lost in his love, was lost. For some in the room, individual differences had trumped the unifying compassion of Christ.

I'm not picking on my dear brothers and friends; I was just surprised to learn they were human too.

Reflection

Unity and Diversity

I believe God gave us all individual differences to trick us into community life. Precise rational thinkers benefit from the balance of those with sensitive hearts when it comes to many important decisions. Neat freaks need messy folks, or they might not ever enjoy eating a chocolate ice cream cone while wearing a white shirt. And messy people need neat freaks to help them get the chocolate out. Extroverted evangelicals are needed to write books on street evangelism. Introverts are needed to write about contemplative prayer and to remind the extroverts of the true goal of their efforts. Put them together and something amazing can happen—evangelism flowing out of a contemplative heart.

Some folks have brains more like Apple Computers. They love icons and simplicity. Others have brains like PCs. Give them an Excel spreadsheet and they can rule the world—or at least figure out how much it would cost to do so. A good university will have a lot of Apple users and PC folks on their faculty. Most days are better with input from both poets and scientists. God seems to want us to need each other. He can be pretty tricky that way.

Even when you get down to something as specific as contemplative prayer, you notice two types of people. Not just at the monastery but across the centuries you encounter champions for both *apophatic* (i.e., without images or thoughts) and *kataphatic* (i.e., with images or thoughts) approaches to contemplative prayer. Somehow I believe the answer to this debate, like almost all others involving theological differences, will be "both and" instead of "either or." Individual differences are to be viewed as an occasion of celebration, not conquest. If a bunch of monks who pray four hours a day can have trouble with this, you can imagine how tough it can be for the rest of us.

163

pprentice Activity
Celebrating Our Differences

Find a quiet place to sit down with God for a few minutes. Ask for his input in determining an important person in your life who gets on your nerves because of an individual difference.

[**Note:** We're not talking about character flaws or personality disorders. Instead, focus on normal personality differences such as: being an extrovert or an introvert, making decisions with one's head or heart, being overly neat versus messy, talking slow or fast; being oriented toward action versus contemplation, thinking like a democrat or a republican, thinking like an Apple computer or a PC.]

After having a person in mind, ask for divine help in coming up with a list of at least five good things about the person's trait that differs from your own. Then try on that trait for a day or more before offering a compliment to the individual because of the benefits of this "difference." Just don't tell them why you picked them for the experiment.

Simmering in Colossians 3:1–17 Continued. Please slowly reread verses 1–5 and then meditatively ponder verse 6:

> On account of these the wrath of God is coming on those who are disobedient.

DAY 21

The Solace of Solitude

There is a sense in which the secret to Jesus' ministry is hidden in the lonely places where he goes to pray—often before dawn.

—Henri Nouwen

I'm a fan of silence. It doesn't take long before noise starts to get on my nerves. But for a lot of folks, I think it's the other way around.

I was raised in a noisy church. The floor squeaked. The piano was loud. The organ was louder. And the praise band could make your ears bleed. If that wasn't bad enough, every so often the citywide fire alarm would go off and cause the stained glass to rattle and those with Scofield Bibles to fear they had missed the rapture. When things did get quiet, it was the cue for one of the ushers to start clipping his fingernails in the vestibule.

One time we had a guest minister who had us experimenting with something that had never been heard in our church. Silence! For several minutes we sat listening for the voice of God. I was spiritually confused. Then I thought I was in heaven. But it was too good to be true. From five rows behind me I heard a loud whisper-shout. "Mark! Mark!"

I peeked out through my squinted eyelids. Sure enough, a college student named Mark was sitting several rows in front of me. I quietly turned to look behind me and saw the source of the punctured silence—a red-faced troublemaker named Marvin.

"Mark!" Marvin sprayed again before delivering his message. "I need to emit a large amount of flatulence!" But Marvin said it more succinctly than that.

Then before you could say "pass the Beano," Marvin proved to over three hundred people that he was anything but a liar. The little respite of silence I had been enjoying was gone with his wind. Like I said, not everyone can handle quiet.

Although I was only about seventeen at the time and not very mature concerning the mysteries of the faith, I knew that Marvin's prophetic utterance was not in the Spirit. Later I began to keep a list of other things I had heard in church that were more likely to be motivated by the flesh than the Spirit. I became particularly fond of compiling prophecy bloopers. (If you are not from a charismatic or Quaker tradition, by "prophecy blooper" I'm referring to someone in a congregation standing up and making a pronouncement that they are attributing directly to the mouth of God, when it is obvious to all present that he had not signed off on the communication.)

One time while sitting in the midst of a large charismatic congregation in Virginia Beach, I watched as a gentleman stood up and proclaimed, "Thus saith the Lord. Just as I was with Abraham leading the children of Israel across the wilderness, so I will be with you."

He sat back down as a conquering hero. Not knowing what to do, the pastor began scratching his head. But the man's wife knew how to handle this. She poked her husband in the ribs and spoke biblical accuracy directly into his left ear. The man popped back up and pronounced, "Thus saith the Lord. I made a mistake. It was Moses."

Another of my favorite prophecy bloopers is also the simplest. A friend told me that he witnessed a woman who stood to her feet and announced on behalf of God, "Yea, verily, I am not in this place!"

I quickly put that one near the top of my list. But the one that helps me get back on track in this discussion has to do with noise. After a long offertory number, a little old lady rose up and proclaimed with great confidence: "Thus saith the Lord, the organ is too loud!"

About seven years after I had heard Marvin announce his intentions, I found myself immersed in the noise of a very demanding seminary program in Southern California. Over the years, the institution had witnessed the heavy toll exacted by its crowded curriculum, so the student life department made many recommendations for us to get away for times of spiritual retreat. To help us locate a retreat center, a list of suggested locations had been included in our orientation materials.

I had never heard of the concept of *spiritual retreat* before. But as the busyness and stress mounted, so did my openness to a two-day mini-vacation with God. I scanned the list of retreat centers that had been provided in the orientation packet and picked one just up the coast in Santa Barbara. About a month passed and the circled date on the calendar finally arrived. I called the retreat center again for directions—just to make sure there wouldn't be any problems. Then my wife and I packed a few things in the trunk of our '72 Celica and headed off.

Most of the drive included a near-breathtaking view of the Pacific from Highway 1 as it snaked its way along the coast. After a couple of hours we turned off from the main road onto a winding lane that meandered under a thick green canopy.

The lush vegetation was so different from anything we were use to seeing in Georgia that the view became surreal, like we had discovered Narnia.

We parked the car next to a sandstone mansion, walked across a pathway of tiny stones, and knocked on a thick wooden door befitting of a castle. After some time, the door swung open, and we were looking in the gentle face of a plain-clad nun. She looked surprised to see us, and asked, "Can I help you?"

When I announced that we had reservations, she politely announced that we did not. But she quickly added that they had just received a cancellation and that we'd be welcome to stay. Totally confused, we stepped inside. She lifted a key from a pegboard on the back of a closet and invited us to follow her upstairs to our room. As we walked up the stone steps to the second floor, she said, "You're very fortunate. It usually takes six to eight weeks to get a reservation here."

I said nothing for fear that my response might get us kicked out. She led us into a bedroom that was larger than our apartment. Soft evening light was flooding in from several oversized windows. I walked over to get a view of a glistening sliver of the Pacific as our host was pointing out the other striking feature of the room, an expansive wood-carved ceiling. Then she showed us our green-tiled bathroom, big enough to accommodate a circus elephant.

Before leaving, our host told us that supper would be served in fifteen minutes downstairs in the large dining room across from the library. As soon as she disappeared, I bolted for my briefcase and dug out my folder with the list of retreat centers and realized my mistake. I had made a reservation for one center and then asked for directions to another. As this sank in, I had the distinct impression that this was no accident. I felt that we were at this special place by divine invitation. A wonderful feeling of expectancy began to bubble up. But being a bit neurotic, I used the phone downstairs to call the other center to explain what had happened and to ask their permission for us to stay put. They graciously complied.

After dinner, my wife and I began to explore the expansive retreat center. In one of the hallways a thin little book caught my attention, a burnt-orange copy of *Out of Solitude* by Henri Nouwen. It was the first time I had seen the word *solitude* on a book cover. I turned it over and read about Nouwen's interest in both psychology—he had studied at the Menninger Foundation—and spirituality. His faculty appointment at Yale Divinity School further established his credibility in my mind. I took the book into the library and read it cover to cover. I took it back to the room and read it again. Some of the passages were so mesmerizing, I would pause, reading each thought five or six times before being able to continue.

> In the lonely place, Jesus finds the courage to follow God's will and not his own; to speak God's words and not his own; to do God's work and not his own. . . .
>
> Somewhere we know that without a lonely place our lives are in danger. Somewhere we know that without silence words lose their meaning, that without listening speaking no longer heals, that without distance closeness cannot cure. Somewhere we know that without a lonely place [solitude] our actions quickly become empty gestures. The careful balance between silence and words, withdrawal and involvement, distance and closeness, solitude and community forms the basis of the Christian life and should be the subject of our most personal attention. . . .
>
> In solitude we discover that our life is not a possession to be defended, but a gift to be shared. It's there we recognize that the healing words we speak are not just our own, but are given to us; that the love we can express is part of a greater love.[1]

I got up the next morning and took the book with me to a breakfast of homemade granola, coffee, and orange juice that had been set out for us in the kitchen. I shared some of my thoughts about the book with my wife, Regina, who agreed that there was something spiritual afoot for us both.

After breakfast I began a slow walk around the grounds, book in hand. I meandered back down the tree-lined lane, through a grove of orange trees, and alongside a moss-lined stream. After a while I discovered a little chapel. I stepped inside as a push of cool air and the smell of candles was leaving the room. When my eyes adjusted to the darkness, I saw it—the breathtaking back wall of the chapel. There behind the communion table was a floor-to-ceiling display of glass squares. Through the clear glass you could see a beautifully gnarled and perfectly framed water oak. The loveliness was so overwhelming that it took a while to see the main attraction. Just inside the glass wall—between the tree and me—stood a magnificent, life-sized crucifix. The visual impact was stunning.

I slowly walked to the front row of the chapel without taking my eyes off of the wooden carving of Christ. I sat down and let the silence envelop me for more than an hour. After a while I sank into the deepest sense of peace I had ever known, and I began to listen to words that bubbled up from deep within. It seemed that most of them were not my own. I felt more loved than at any other point in my life. I felt deep joy. I didn't want to leave.

But eventually I gave in to the flesh—my body's finite capacity for storing coffee. I left that chapel, still holding a copy of *Out of Solitude*, forever changed by the love whispered to me in silence.

Reflection

Listening to the Silence

When I say that weekend changed my life, I'm not giving in to hyperbole. In the years that followed, the desire to practice as a psychologist—in a traditional manner—gradually eroded, giving ground to a growing interest in spiritual direction. My wife and I spent an entire year visiting retreat centers. I invested over thirty days in going through a traditional Ignatian retreat, and the past two decades have been pretty much consumed by the desire to experience and share with others more of the joyous mysteries mined from the silence and solitude of that initial retreat. So what was happening?

According to James Connor in *Silent Fire*, embracing *silence* is "the one door into communion with God."[2] Drawing on the wisdom of Thomas Merton, Connor discusses "four circles of silence."

The first circle of silence is entered when we decide to retreat from noise and words. Retreat centers offer environments where it is possible to experience this circle. La Casa de Maria was the setting where for the first time in my life prayer became more than a soliloquy of complaints or requests. During that time of taking little vacations from human words, the opportunity to better hear divine whispers was greatly facilitated.

The second circle of silence, according to Connor and Merton, is the realm where we allow thoughts to fade away, at least for a little while. The first time I experienced this—other than occasions of momentarily becoming lost between daydreams—was during a thirty-day Ignatian at the Stella Maris Retreat Center in Upstate New York. If you are not familiar with this type of structured retreat, it involves, at least in part, spending four to six hours a day meditating on select passages of Scripture.

For one of these meditation sessions, I was sitting in the empty chapel after Mass. The room was filled with what had become the comforting smell of burning candles and old lectionaries. From the large windows at the front I could see the easternmost part of the Finger Lakes. While I don't remember the passage I was reading, I do remember sinking into a deep silence and seeing—at the back of my closed eyelids—what seemed to be a universe of empty space. This awareness was followed by a gradual cessation of thoughts. I remember thinking about not thinking briefly and then the gentle pleasure of letting that thought go and the profound realization that there is something in me that lies beneath and beyond my thoughts.

In a few thought-free times that have followed, I have come to believe that there is a real me that is much more than my thoughts. The real me—that silence is beginning to reveal—is most often hidden behind a vale of noise, inner chatter, and ego. The real me longs for nothing more than the fulfillment of Jesus' prayer in John 17:21, to melt into the union of love that is the Trinity.

The third and forth circles of silence (a deeper sense of having no self apart from God and deep contemplation, respectively) are beyond the scope of this discussion—and beyond what I can discuss from repeated personal experience. However, I can say that from my first accidental encounter with silence and solitude and across two decades of repeated forays, it is in silence that I have heard most clearly God's life-giving whispers of love and experienced most deeply a sense of identity as God's beloved.

pprentice Activity
Silent Movie and Minutes

If you are unable to schedule a silent retreat, rent a copy of the award-winning documentary *Into Great Silence* and spend a few hours pondering what it means when it is reported in 1 Kings 19:11b–12, "But the LORD was not in the wind: and after the wind an earthquake; but the LORD was not in the earthquake: and after the earthquake a fire; but the LORD was not in the fire: and after the fire a still small voice" (KJV).

Simmering in Colossians 3:1–17 Continued. Please slowly reread verses 1–6 and then meditatively ponder verse 7:

These are the ways you also once followed, when you were living that life.

22

If God Is So Smart, Why Am I Doing All the Talking?

Why is it that when we speak to God we are said to be praying but when God speaks to us we are said to be schizophrenic?

—Lily Tomlin

It is presumptuous and dangerous to undertake human existence without hearing God.

—Dallas Willard

My uncle Otis was born in 1919. He was one of nine children, all raised on a dairy farm just outside Waycross, Georgia. If you're over thirty-five years old and you've had brushes with the Pentecostal world, you may have attended one of his revivals. You'd remember. Otis was one of a kind: bigger than life, love on two feet, and in constant

173

motion—an old school, Holy Ghost evangelist. The kind who made demons sweat and angels laugh.

A friend of Otis's once asked him, "How did someone as energetic as you keep from being bored when you were a boy growing up on a dairy farm?"

"That's easy," he answered, "I'd just grab a bull by the tail and hold on."

"Didn't that hurt?"

"Not if you didn't let go."

That was my uncle. He grabbed hold of life and refused to let it go. He was all in, all the time.

Several stories about Otis have stained my brain. For example, I was told that once while Otis was on a crusade in Haiti he heard there was a local witch doctor working against his revival effort. He and a pastor-friend decided to attend the voodoo service the spiritual practitioner was conducting. They sat on the back row and prayed.

After a struggle in the heavenlies, which could be seen in the witch doctor's halting motions, he finally declared that he had to stop the ceremony. "I don't understand it," he began, "but there is a power present that's greater than mine and it's working against me. I have to stop."

That's when Uncle Otis jumped to his feet and announced, "That's just us back here praying to Jesus."

Occasionally things did get a little confusing. Once when casting out a demon, Uncle Otis said, "What's your name?"

"Lie," said the demon.

"Are you telling me the truth, lying demon?" Uncle Otis shot back.

I'm not sure how that particular demon responded to such a double bind—he may have gone off shaking his head and looking for a herd of pigs. But I am confident he knew he had met a confounding opponent.

People placed a lot of confidence in Uncle Otis's faith too. Out of the blue, a man approached him in the hallway of a hotel once and said, "I've got a physical problem and need you to pray for me."

"What is it?" Otis asked.

"Constipation," the man whispered sheepishly.

"Well, let's pray right now," Uncle Otis bellowed. Then he put his big paw on the man's forehead and shouted, "Be healed of this constipation, instantly!"

I'm not sure how the results came out, but I'm pretty confident the man felt better: if for no other reason than not making his request to Otis in front of a crowded auditorium.

At Uncle Otis's funeral, one of his friends said with a smile, "Otis has never been accused of preaching." It was a humorous way of referring to the fact that Otis the evangelist wasn't effective because of cleverly crafted words artistically strung across a three-point outline. No, Otis never offered his audience revelation of obscure truth mined from Greek verb tenses. He offered them instead the words he'd heard God whisper into his ear during their unceasing conversations. That was the secret to his success as an evangelist. He grabbed his relationship with God by the tail and never let go. Let me rephrase that. Otis spent his adult life abiding with the one he loved. He knew that is what it took to hear the voice of God. And he wasn't timid about passing on what he had heard to others.

I miss my uncle. He was an original.

Reflection

Living in Conversation with God

Dallas Willard is an original too. But as far as I can discern, he only has three things in common with my uncle Otis. Stature—both physical and spiritual—southern roots, and the belief that it is possible to live life so close to God that you can hear his voice. Dallas says it best in his wonderful book, *Hearing God: Developing a Conversational Relationship with God*:

"People are meant to live in an ongoing conversation with God, speaking and being spoken to."[1] The way God visited with Adam and Enoch is to become routine for us. After all, "God created us for intimate friendship with himself—both now and forever."[2]

For many people—but certainly not Otis and Dallas—hearing God can be like an infrequently played parlor game or stopping to ask for directions after finally admitting to being lost. Or worse yet, it can be left to another individual to do on our behalf. I'll never forget having someone approach me while I was praying at an altar to say, "God has a word for you." After relaying what that "word" was—and it turned out to be more of a long paragraph—I remember being flattered and a little confused. What I did not say at the time was, "Why do you think God would interrupt the conversation we were in the middle of to have you tell me something for him? We were already talking!"

The point is, hearing God doesn't make much sense except within the context of living life a certain kind of way, the way of constant, ongoing, interactive friendship. The way of John 17:3: "And this is eternal life, that they may know you, the only true God, and Jesus Christ whom you have sent" (NRSV). We best hear God through *knowing* him—the process of being mutually indwelt, one within the other—in a passionate relationship in which conversation is but one facet. In such a transforming friendship with God, communication includes more than an exchange of words. It advances into deeper communion and consummation.

Again, Dallas says it best:

> Human beings were once alive to God. They were created to be responsive to and interactive with him. Adam and Eve lived in conversational relationship with their Creator, daily renewed. But when they mistrusted God and disobeyed him, that cut them off from the realm of

176

the Spirit. *They became as dead to the realm of the Spirit as a kitten is dead to arithmetic.*[3]

And, Dallas continues . . .

In the purpose of God's redemptive work *communication* advances into *communion* and communion into *union*. When the progression is complete we can truly say, "It is no longer I who live, but it is Christ who lives in me."(Galatians 2:20) and "For me, living is Christ" (Phil. 1:21).[4]

Both Uncle Otis and Dallas Willard agree. The goal is not hearing God. The goal is the enjoyment of a perpetual and transforming friendship.

pprentice Activity
Listening for the Voice of God

The still small voice of God that speaks, the quiet inner whisper, is a highly valuable form for God to communicate his purposes. But it is best heard when we are orchestrating each day in such a way that we are constantly abiding in his presence: experiencing salvation as an exciting journey toward union with God—not a legal transaction (Day 13); no longer "yada, yada, yada-ing" salvation, but instead celebrating the spiritual romance of "knowing" God (Day 14); routinely stepping into Holy Sacraments such as communion, baptism, and sunny Wednesday afternoons to experience the mystery of Christ within (Days 15 & 16); slowing down to allow Scripture to read us (Days 17 & 18); enjoying both the unity (Day 19) and diversity (Day 20) of others; and spending time in the circles of silence and solitude (Day 21) on a routine basis. Against that backdrop, the mystery of hearing God's voice can become marvelously mundane.

Against the backdrop of all the above, hearing God's voice becomes more commonplace and we can become less confused about whether or not we've heard from God, the thief and robber, or last night's pizza.

Following your time of silence today, ask God a few direct questions (e.g., "What do you think of me?" or "What would you like for us to do together today?" etc.), and if you hear a response, then ask yourself two questions:

1. Did what I heard sound more like the voice of a gentle shepherd or a loud cattle driver?
2. Was the emotional impact one of increased love, peace, joy, and certainty or anger, fear, despair, and confusion?

Note: If you could answer "shepherd" to number 1 and check off any of the fruit of the Spirit and a sense of certainty on number 2, I believe the chances are much higher you heard from God.

Simmering in Colossians 3:1–17 Continued. Please slowly reread verses 1–7 and then meditatively ponder verse 8:

> But now you must get rid of all such things—anger, wrath, malice, slander, and abusive language from your mouth.

Carrying On
the Master's Legacy

Jesus Living through Me

Medieval apprenticeship programs were not only the first step toward becoming a master, but also preliminary to citizenship in the city where the master lived. The process was carefully controlled and regulated—including the initiation.

Late medieval society, being largely still an oral culture, retained a suspicion that the written word was not adequate for important matters, such as becoming an initiate into the mysteries of a craft. As a consequence, the act of entering into apprenticeship required solemn ceremonies with many witnesses in order to impress on the mind of the youth and those around him that he had taken a major step, with obligations and implications for his life for the next seven to ten or more years. One remembered obligations better when rituals reinforced them.[1]

After the contract was signed and the initiation completed, the journey toward becoming a master was under way. Each step would involve hands-on experiences working beside the teacher, until it was as if the master was working *through* the apprentice.

As we have discussed, the basic nature of the relationship between a rabbi and disciple mirrors a medieval apprenticeship program—or perhaps given the calendar it would be better to say it the other way around. This basic rabbi/disciple model was retained by Jesus and his disciples. It is both profoundly powerful and simple. Jesus' disciples were learning to be like him by being "with him." They were literally where he was and progressively involved in doing what he was doing.

But what about after Jesus' death and resurrection, did that model continue with the apostles becoming the "masters"? Yes and no. They became masters in the sense that they gathered people and told stories about Jesus and life in the kingdom; they showed by example what it looked like to be living life with Jesus in the real world. But, because of the resurrection and through the gift of the Spirit of Christ, it was possible for Jesus to continue serving as the true master. And still is. This is what Paul meant in Colossians 1:26–27: "The mystery that has been kept hidden for ages and generations, but is now disclosed to the saints. . . . Christ in you, the hope of glory."

For both the first-century church and the twenty-first-century church, the practice of discipleship is an experience of apprenticeship. It is a matter of learning to be like Jesus by being with those who are further along the same path, but it is more than that. It is learning to be like Jesus by being with the resurrected Christ. And, it is even much more than that! It is learning to allow him to live his life through us. This, of course, ultimately requires a progressive death to the ego self, the part of us that continues to desire autonomy and self-rule. It requires the embrace of a personal cross. It is the end to a nominal approach to Christianity.

The central theme of this section on carrying on the Master's legacy is learning to allow Jesus to live his life through me. This is the most painful section as the focus shifts to the personal cross—less of me, more of thee. The topics covered include: letting go of self-sufficiency (Day 23); developing trust and companionship (Day 24); learning from dark nights of the soul (Day 25) and other painful life experiences (Day 26); addressing the need to slow down (Day 27); and "eating" a balanced diet (Day 28). The section concludes with reflections on becoming a master craftsman (Day 29) and apprenticing others (Day 30).

Invitation to Join the Guild

Letting Go of Self-Sufficiency

It's better to admit you are a mutt than to pretend to be a poodle.

—Curt Cloninger

Are you a dog person or a cat person? I'm a dog person myself. I never had much use for cats. That's probably because I never met a cat that had much use for me.

Cats are Pharisees. They're snooty, care too much about appearances, and don't need anyone but themselves. In fact, about the only good thing you can say about cats is that they're clean. But when a cat is trying to dislodge a hairball, I confess to having rooted for the hairball.

Now dogs are a completely different matter. Most every dog I've been around has acted like a fine Christian.

I got my first dog when I was five years old. My family moved for the fifth time in as many years, and I was trying to adjust to school and a new neighborhood. Right in the middle of the crisis, I remember going to sleep on the sofa, in tears.

The next thing I knew, a brown and black ball of fur was licking me awake. It took me about two seconds to forget about my problems. I named my new best friend Frisky—I got the name off of the first can of animal food I saw that night and later had to apologize to Frisky when I realized I'd named him after a cat.

That night I went to sleep with my hand on Frisky's back. I'd just known him for a day, but he'd taught me a valuable lesson. It doesn't take much to make someone feel better—just show up and let them know how glad you are to see them.

A year later we moved again and Frisky fell in with the wrong crowd and didn't come back home. Actually, I think he got killed, because we'd become pretty good buddies and liked being together each day. I wasn't much good to anyone for about a month.

It was a long time before I wanted another dog. By the time I decided it was worth the risk, I was in college taking Hebrew. I named the new pet Kelev, which is Hebrew for "dog." I think the joke was lost on Kelev. And if I had it to do over, I would have named him Kitty. Standing out in the backyard saying, "Here, Kitty, Kitty, Kitty," only to have a giant, mostly German shepherd gallop up would be a joke everybody would get.

To be honest, by the time Kelev came along, I had discovered the opposite sex and Kelev became a neglected pet. But he never complained. Anytime I had a minute for him, he just smiled and enjoyed the time with me. I learned a lot about forgiveness from Kelev.

My next experience with dogs came long after I was married and had a couple of children. I had resisted getting a family dog—I think in part because of the bittersweet experiences I'd had with pets. But that didn't keep someone from dropping off a couple of stray mutts at our house.

Those two dogs were pretty smart. Or, to be more precise, one was gifted and the other was a follower. One morning a newspaper—unchewed and in a red plastic bag—had been dragged from my neighbor's yard to the driver's side of my car; the two dogs sat beside it waiting for me to see the present. That evening a dog dish showed up in our yard. I asked my wife if she had decided we should keep the dogs. But she hadn't bought the dish. Turns out the dogs had borrowed it from the same neighbor. There was no mistake in their meaning. For a little food, they would stay at our house and be on call twenty-four hours a day.

We let those two dogs hang out at our place for as long as they wanted. We did buy them their own dish and made them return the one they'd "borrowed." And in the years that followed, they taught us a lot of lessons about sensitivity, forgiveness, loyalty, and the joy of being alive in the present moment. I do hope that someday I'll be as good a person as my dogs have always believed that I was.

I have a friend who likes mutts too. His name is Curt Cloninger. He's a comedian. But I think he's the type of comedian Mark Twain must have had in mind when he said, "Show me someone who can make you laugh and I'll show you someone who can make you cry."

One of Curt's alter egos is from my part of the rural south. His name is Bubba Johnson. I've gotten Curt's permission to tell you one of his stories. While I'm pretty sure this didn't really happen, make no mistake, where Curt and I are from, it could have. And it makes an important point about being an apprentice to Jesus.

According to Curt, Bubba was sitting around his tire store with some of his friends one day eating MoonPies and washing them down with RC Colas. With all that sugar, things got pretty deep. The group began to ponder some of the most important philosophical questions, such as: "What do you think God likes best, dogs or cats?" There was immediate unanimity among the boys: dogs.

When a more complex question arose, "Which do you think God likes best, mutts or purebreds?" Bubba ended the discussion by declaring, "God likes mutts best, because that's just the nature of God."

Then Bubba went on to tell others about someone he knew named Raymond Boley and his dog, Partner. Raymond was a chicken rancher who was very fond of his pickup truck. He kept it spotless. Even the engine block was so clean you could grill chickens on it, if you wanted to. So, it was very curious to Bubba that Raymond would let his mutt-dog ride in the cab and drool all over the leather upholstery.

When Bubba inquired, Raymond told him the background story.

A while back Raymond was having some trouble with his chicken houses. He kept hearing noises during the night and waking up to see the remains of some of his chickens outside the houses. Some form of critter was getting in and going through the buffet line of birds.

Raymond's wife, Earline, suggested that they get a watch-dog. And then she suggested that it be a pure-blooded poodle. She reasoned that if you have a watchdog, it might as well be one that doesn't shed and looks pretty on the sofa. Earline was a persuasive woman.

The first night after bringing the watch-poodle home, Raymond heard noises again. He rushed outside with his shotgun and opened fire. *Blam!* Problem solved. Then Raymond returned to his house to find the poodle still on the couch, not shedding.

A few days later Raymond went to the pound to get him a real dog with some street smarts. He looked around and locked eyes with a pitiful pooch and instantly decided that it was the dog for him.

When he told the man who ran the pound, he just laughed and said, "You don't want that worthless mutt!"

"I do," Raymond insisted.

"No, you don't. We're just holding him for four days because the state says we have to, but we're going to gas that worthless mutt."

"No, I want that dog!"

"No, you don't."

"Yes, I do."

"You do not want that dog. He's full of buckshot!"

About that time a lightbulb turned on in Raymond's head. He walked over, bent down, and stroked the dog. Sure enough, he was full of buckshot. Raymond pulled his lips back. Chicken feathers!

Raymond stood up slowly and said with great certainty, "I tell you something. I'm choosing that one. That's going to be my dog."

So Raymond Boley paid pretty big bucks to hock that mutt out of the pound and even bigger bucks to the vet for patching him up. Then he took it home, fed him, forgave him, and named him Partner. And Partner returned the favor by becoming the most loyal friend and watchdog Raymond ever knew.

So, Bubba's Bible made easy:

1. God loves mutts and loves to forgive them.
2. It's better to admit you are a mutt than pretend you are a poodle.
3. Only forgiven mutts get to ride shotgun in God's pickup truck.

Reflection

Amazing Grace

Do you ever think you are not good enough for an apprenticeship program with God? Do you think he might pick someone, but not you? Well, keep in mind that God loves mutts.

Just think about the lowbrows Jesus chose to invest his life in. There was a common fisherman named Peter whom the Sanhedrin (a famous collection of poodles in Jesus' day) suggested was "unlearned and ignorant" (Acts 4:12 KJV). Another had been a student of a camel-skin-wearing, locust-eating hermit, completely unschooled in rabbinical matters. Yet Jesus trusted him to write five books of the New Testament. Another was a despised tax collector; another famous only for his doubts; and yet another was best known for being the host of seven demons (Mark 16:9). The bottom line is, they were mutts—rabbi school discards—one and all.

It wasn't any better in the Old Testament. In fact, the Bible itself begins with two ugly divorces (the fall of Satan and the fall of humanity) before things get worse. One brother kills another. Surviving a flood is celebrated by getting drunk and then naked. A birthright is stolen—by the "good guy." The most famous patriarch lies under pressure. And when a hero finally appears, he's a murderer. Yet the whole book becomes the story of God loving his mutts and trying to win them, win us, back.

But that's not even the most important point. Lots of folks know they are mutts—at least deep down inside—but they pretend to be something more. They hope that if they can just do enough or earn enough or have enough, they can earn God's acceptance. They are pretending to be poodles. And therein we find a major off-ramp for the apprenticeship program being described. Becoming an apprentice requires more than being with Jesus; it ultimately requires us to allow him to live his life through us. And that requires a personal cross, a place where all pretence of self-sufficiency must die.

pprentice Activity
Burn the Doubts and Then Give Up

Get a note pad, pen, and about thirty minutes. Write down every reason you can think of for being unworthy to continue this apprenticeship program with Jesus. Don't be nice to yourself and don't leave anything out. Tell God why you shouldn't participate.

Then, after a time of silence before God, ask him if he's sure you are fit for the program. Listen carefully for his response.

Then let him know that the only way you can become his apprentice, to live your life as he would live it, is to give up all pretense of self-sufficiency, and pray that he will live his life through you.

Simmering in Colossians 3:1–17 Continued. Please slowly reread verses 1–8 and then meditatively ponder verse 9:

Do not lie to one another, seeing that you have stripped off the old self with its practices.

24

Trust and Companionship

Another Lesson in Surrender

Abraham had to empty his heart. . . . And when he did so, he made room for God's abundant blessing. He became a friend of God through surrender.

—Joshua Kang, *Deep-Rooted in Christ*

We were in the Marriot Hotel in downtown Atlanta. To my left was Heidi, an accomplished editor. To my right was Charlie Shedd, the author of over forty books who often had been affectionately referred to as the "Pope of the Presbyterian Church." The occasion was the fact that Charlie and I both had books coming out with the same publisher, and the company thought it would be a good thing if its longtime and first-time author got to know each other, especially since we lived so close—separated by only about twenty-five miles of two-lane road.

When the meal arrived I was not surprised to hear the "Pope" say, "Let's thank the Lord." But I was taken aback when Charlie brought the waiter in on the sacred moment:

"We always pray before we eat," Charlie says to the waiter. He nods.

"Would you like to join us?"

The waiter swallows hard.

"I like to hold hands while asking the blessing," Charlie continues. "Would you like to be part of the circle?"

I swallow hard.

The waiter sheepishly takes Charlie's outthrust hand and then Heidi's. I look at the waiter who is trying to say without words to his waiter friends, "I don't know these people."

But Charlie is not through. "Now," he says to the waiter while we are all holding hands in a Kumbaya circle in a four-star dining room, "would you like to pray for us?"

After a few moments of awkward silence, the waiter launches into a beautiful blessing.

As he is leaving our table, Heidi asks Charlie, "Do you do that often?"

"No."

"Have you ever done that before?"

"No."

"Well, that was odd, Charlie, very odd!"

"What do you think about Charlie's odd behavior, Gary? You're a psychologist, do you think you can help him?"

"Well, I only met him twenty minutes ago, so you are asking for a very quick diagnosis. But my initial impression is that Charlie does seem a bit odd here, but good odd, God odd."

"What?"

"Psychologists are in the business of helping people become more normal, less odd. But I think Jesus was in the business of getting people to be odd. He didn't want his followers to fit in this world, he wanted them to be at home in the kingdom. And the ways of the kingdom are often at odds with those of the world. I think if we are going to be like Jesus, we're often going to look pretty odd to the world—oddly loving, oddly peaceful, oddly joyful. Just like Charlie, here."

Silence.

The conversation returned to normal, and the three of us enjoyed a leisurely meal.

At 3 a.m. I was awakened from a deep sleep by a phone call. After multiple rings I pick it up. It's Charlie. He's wide awake and way too chipper for an eighty-two-year-old man.

"Gary, I've been thinking about what you said, about what it would mean to be as odd as Jesus, every minute of the day. I need to talk with someone about this right now. Can you meet me in the lobby in five minutes?"

"Charlie, you do know that all 'odd' isn't 'God-odd,' don't you?"

But it was too late; he'd already hung up the phone. I met Charlie in the lobby and within an hour we'd hammered out the ideas for doing a book together to be called *I'm Odd, Thank God.*

For the next two years Charlie and I got together two or three times each month at Charlie's mini-farm just outside Athens, Georgia, to spend the day working on that book idea. If the truth were known, I didn't care that much about the book; I was just delighted to be in a mentoring relationship with a famous writer.

Like Charlie himself, his house was warm and inviting. It was filled with cabinets, tables, and bookcases that he had made in his woodshop. And even though his much beloved wife, Martha, had passed away a few years prior, the walls, decorations, and photo albums kept her personality alive in each room.

Outside the big yellow house there was a red barn and a large, fenced-in corral. Charlie's woodshop was in half the barn. The other half was where another one of his hobbies resided—a prize-winning mule.

I loved walking with Charlie around his backyard. That's where he would tell me his animal stories. Inside the house, the genre would change. Sitting around the kitchen table or in the den is where Charlie played the highlight reels from the parts of his life shared with human beings. He loved to relive his childhood, his early courtship with Martha, college pranks, seminary days, his fascination with the Gullah culture, squabbles with deacon boards, and ministry successes. And when we were done with all the important stuff, we'd work on the book about being odd for God.

As I'm typing these words, I hear a friend in the hallway use the word "providence." This is a word that always makes me think "Presbyterian." And before you can say "John Calvin," a memory from my time with Charlie begins playing in my head like a scene from a movie.

I remember that about a year into the writing apprenticeship, I asked Charlie a question.

"Charlie, I know a lot of people have called you the 'Pope of the Presbyterian Church,' especially during your time as pastor of the Memorial Drive Church in Houston. But we've spent a lot of time together and I don't think I've ever heard you mention John Calvin. What's up with that?"

"Well, Gary, it's like this. I read somewhere that Calvin suffered a lot from kidney stones."

I waited for him to continue. When it was obvious he was finished with that odd sentence, I said, "So . . ."

"Well, it occurred to me that John Calvin wrote theology like a man suffering from kidney stones."

While I'm careful not to share that story with anyone wearing a Calvin College sweatshirt, that memory and a few hundred more have become permanently planted in my brain as a result of all the time I spent with Charlie. Each day now, I can count on something happening that will trigger one of these memories to play in my head.

All of my memories with Charlie are not pleasant. There was something that happened while we were working on the book together that brings back bittersweet emotions.

Our plan was for Charlie to tell me life stories. I would listen, take notes, and bring them back in written form. For our book, Charlie was to be the star in a semi-biography about a man who lived his life "Odd for God." I was his apprentice, learning how to write and live more like Charlie.

Each week I would read to Charlie what I had written. He would offer critique for my writing style, add some facts, and then tell fresh stories. The next week I'd bring back a second draft and most often he would lavish praise on the new creation, expressing approval with a loud, "That's my boy!" I loved it! It was as if I'd won the lottery.

After about a year, we were done. A two-hundred-page manuscript was ready to be sent off to the publisher. Charlie's life, my words, it was the best thing I'd ever done. Visions of a bestseller were dancing in my head.

But by this time I had begun to notice some things about Charlie—especially what seemed to be declining memory and judgment—that had made me wonder if he was beginning to step back behind a thin curtain of dementia.

To my surprise, instead of telling me to send the manuscript in, Charlie wanted us to go back through it, to keep whittling away. Since I was mostly into the process for the time with Charlie, I signed on for round two. But as the months went by, it became clear that Charlie was indeed beginning to lose portions of the self that he had been. As those months turned into a second year, the manuscript I had been so proud of was slowly being reshaped into something I could barely recognize. The cloudy curtain of dementia was becoming thicker.

At the end of the second year, Charlie moved to Oklahoma. We had a farewell lunch at his favorite restaurant. I told him how grateful I was for all the time we'd shared. We laughed and reminisced. As he was leaving, I gave him both versions of the manuscript (the two-hundred-page original and the forty-page rewrite) and told him that just being with him was reward enough.

"You keep working on this and don't turn it loose until you are ready. It's all yours and I hope you have another million-copy bestseller."

Charlie died a couple of years later. But before he did, a publisher friend—who knew the full story and commiserated with me often—published Charlie's last book (number 40, I believe) titled *I'm Odd, Thank You God.*

Reflection

Less of Me, More of You

I was hesitant to tell this story. I will always believe that the best version of our book—the one written before Charlie stepped behind the curtain—was not published. But I tell it because I think that in the end it became a good and positive story. While there is a small part of me that wishes it had a different ending, it's not my best part. The best part is grateful for the gift of time—for the apprenticeship—that Charlie gave me. In the end, the trust and companionship outweighed any disappointments.

While we did not collaborate on a bestseller, my friend Charlie is alive inside my head. It's rare I type a sentence without hearing him say, "Remember, Gary, keep the sentences short." Or "Never use the same word twice in a sentence"; "Keep it moving"; "Always use picturesque speech"; "Don't state the obvious—of course he fell *down*, where else could he fall?"; "No one cares about you but your mother, talk to the reader about the reader." Like all good mentors, Charlie planted words and ideas that live on. I see clearly now that the goal was, not the product, but the process of transformation.

I can also see the important similarity in becoming an apprentice to Jesus. When I am able to allow old dreams to be shattered, new visions emerge. To the extent that I can become empty of ego self, the great mystery of Christ within and living-through is revealed.

pprentice Activity
Becoming Empty of Self and Full of God

Surely God's heart was full of love for his only Son. But he emptied his heart for our sakes. In turn, Christ emptied himself and became one of us. The first Patriarch of the church placed his own Son on the altar, emptying his heart temporarily of his love for his own Son. Jesus' disciples began their journeys with him by letting go of all else.

Take a few minutes to talk with God about your own journey of transformation. If you feel frustrated by your progress or inspired by the thought that spiritual formation begins with emptiness, ask God to reveal to you what may need to be placed on the altar.

Simmering in Colossians 3:1–17 Continued. Please slowly reread verses 1–9 and then meditatively ponder verse 10:

> and have clothed yourselves with the new self, which is being renewed in knowledge according to the image of its creator.

DAY
25

Getting through the Rough Spots
The Importance of Dark Nights of the Soul

For as the surest source of destruction to men is to obey themselves, so the only haven of safety is to have no other will, no
other wisdom, than to follow the Lord wherever he leads. Let
this, then, be the first step, to abandon ourselves, and devote
the whole energy of our minds to the service of God.

—John Calvin

In my own personal apprenticeship program I very often
encounter rough spots; I live in ongoing vacillation between
cruising down the highway "with God" and being stuck in
the mire of self-determination. I often wonder if I'll ever see
progress again. But I have learned a couple of things along
the way that have proven to be helpful in such times. I learned
one from a couple of laboratory rats and the other from a

197

gay friend. I'll start with the rats, but the stories are really interrelated.

I was introduced to psychology during the halcyon days of behaviorism. Everywhere you looked in the university's psychology department, pigeons were playing ping-pong and rats were running mazes.

Two of the rats were pretty smart. They taught me something very profound about addiction. The first lived in a small wire house. The only furniture was a water tube and a lever. Every time he pressed the lever, a food pellet appeared. It was more convenient than a McDonald's drive-through.

But then one day something cruel happened. He pressed but no pellets. He pressed again. No pellets. He pressed it like a telegraph operator. No pellets. And when no one wearing a white coat offered to fix the machine, he returned to his lever pressing with greater resolve. But time passed. The pressing became less frequent. Eventually he gave up and went back to his former job.

Another rat in the neighborhood lived in a very different house—probably designed by Stephen King. A small but painful current of electricity ran through the wire floor of his cage that caused him to bounce around wildly. When one of his leaps caused him to land on a lever, the current stopped—for a little while. Eventually he grasped the connection and began to press the lever to make his pain go away.

However, one day a sadistic psychologist decided to leave the current turned on no matter what the rat did. The rat panicked and started pressing the lever like a hummingbird on crack. We thought he'd never stop. Before he finally gave up, he had pressed that bar far more times and for a much longer period of time than his neighbor.

What's the point? There are two. Negative reinforcement—increasing a behavior by taking away something painful—is far more powerful than positive reinforcement—increasing a behavior by adding something positive. Second, addictive behavior often follows the more powerful negative reinforcement paradigm. When a person discovers that a substance or behavior pattern can stop pain, it can be a very difficult thing to unlearn.

I have a friend who developed an addiction to alcohol. He grew up in a small town. He attended a Bible-believing church. His parents were pillars of the community. But his life became a grid of painful shocks.

By the time he was in the third grade, he had begun to feel different from his friends. By the time he was in the fifth grade, he knew what it was. He was gay. It was a secret he would keep hidden until his early forties. Each day of his life brought fresh jolts of electricity.

Unfortunately, in his early twenties he found a liquid way to stop the pain—at least for a while. And it wasn't long until one drink a day had become twelve. Negative reinforcement is a powerful thing.

Time passed and things got worse. A few years ago he was in a car accident that crushed his foot and left him with chronic physical pain. Within a few months, his best friend died and his family discovered his secret. They wrote him off as a lost cause. Soon the beer turned to Vodka and happy hour began at 10:00 a.m. each day.

It took a DUI conviction and a night in jail to get him to his first AA meeting. He drove to it with an open can of beer between his legs. But around the seventh meeting something clicked and he took the first of the twelve steps. He admitted his powerlessness and turned his life over to God. That was three years ago. He went home and poured out gallons of liquor. For the past three years he has lived a celibate life and enjoys his new family—an AA group in his neighborhood.

My friend's remarkable journey reminds me of something Dallas Willard wrote in *Renovation of the Heart*. "Any successful plan for spiritual formation . . . will in fact be significantly similar to the Alcoholics Anonymous program."[1]

I'm proud of my friend. He's found a healthy way to stop most of his painful shocks. He is experiencing what Dallas described as foundational to formation: willing and radical surrender to God, community support, ruthless honesty, and accountability. I just wish he had been able to find those answers in church.

Reflection
Proper Use of Pain

What does all this have to do with getting through the rough spots of an apprenticeship program? Being an apprentice to Jesus involves living out a very deep level of trust and surrender. A great threat to living at such levels of "letting go" is what we've learned from living in our own wire cages. That is to say, for most folks, life has involved a lot of painful shocks to the system. So we bounce around like laboratory rats and eventually stumble onto things that help to deaden the pain. These painkillers may take the form of certain patterns of behavior—like perfectionism, overachievement, approval seeking, avoidance, people pleasing, codependence, always being right, being in control, etc.—and they make take the form of abusing some substance that helps to deaden the pain. Regardless of the form, these God-substitutes are, simply put, "idols" often established in our lives through negative reinforcement.

For me, most of my rough spots during an ongoing apprenticeship with God end up being caused by my turning away from living my life "with-God" and returning to patterns of coping that are under my control. For me, the way through the rough spots always parallels the path taken by my friend and significantly resemble the steps of Alcoholics Anonymous: confession of my addiction to self-sufficiency, admission of my helplessness to live a meaningful life on my own terms, and a whispered request to return to living life by God's side—who has always welcomed me back to his side with a warm embrace.

200

While it is beyond the scope of our discussion, I should reference another common "rough spot" faced by apprentices. Devotion masters—dating back to St. John of the Cross—have talked about it, using the label "dark night of the soul." During the dryness of an emotional dark night, we also feel the pain of separation from God. Our apprenticeship is not going smoothly, but for a very different reason than what was described above. We have not returned to trusted idols; in fact, we cannot figure out what, if anything, we are doing wrong. The pain of a dark night experience is the pain of a perceived absence. For a period of time it's as if God quits showing up.

As I discussed in another book, *Falling for God*:

> All believers who want to become an apprentice of Christ and not just his admirer will find themselves in the blank space between the verses in Psalm 23. Because he loves us so much, the Shepherd moves on. We look around and wonder where he has gone. We feel alone, abandoned. We call out. Nothing. The voice that used to call our name is silent and does not respond when we call. He is gone. He has moved farther down the road that leads home. During the dark night experience our job is to seek God and to go to him again. When we do, we realize we are not the same person. Our relationship with him is not the same. We [too] have moved. We are closer to home and closer to union.[2]

So whether my rough spot is due to me moving toward idols or God moving me on down the path to greater maturity, my job, your job, remains the same. We say, "Here I am, Lord, helpless without you."

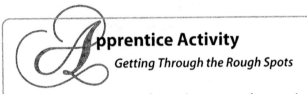

pprentice Activity
Getting Through the Rough Spots

When you become aware of a rough spot—a real or perceived break in the relationship between apprentice and master—slowly read the words from John Calvin below and then breathe the following prayer for fifteen to twenty minutes before taking it with you through the rest of the day.

> For as the surest source of destruction to men is to obey themselves, so the only haven of safety is to have no other will, no other wisdom, than to follow the Lord wherever he leads. Let this, then, be the first step, to abandon ourselves, and devote the whole energy of our minds to the service of God.[3]

[As you inhale] "With God"
[As you exhale] "For joy"
[As you inhale] "With God"
[As you exhale] "At a slow pace"

Simmering in Colossians 3:1–17 Continued. Please slowly reread verses 1–10 and then meditatively ponder verse 11:

> In that renewal there is no longer Greek and Jew, circumcised and uncircumcised, barbarian, Scythian, slave and free; but Christ is all and in all!

DAY 26

Working with the Proper Light

And Letting It Pour In through the Cracks in My Façade

We must imitate Christ's life and his ways if we are to be truly enlightened and set free from the darkness of our own hearts. Let it be the most important thing we do, then, to reflect on the life of Jesus Christ.

—Thomas à Kempis

Donald Harris is a remarkable man. While serving as a Navy chaplain, he developed an affinity for outcast sailors, finding himself drawn to those who repulsed most others—the abused and the abusers, the afflicted and the addicted, the yellers and the smashers. Hollow, angry eyes were, for him, a siren call for grace. But the young lieutenant had a major problem. The ones who most needed his help often had hearts of stone—impenetrable to his offer of God's love.

It wasn't long until Chaplain Harris got an idea. Music! He began to wonder what would happen if he cloaked his message in song. A stealth missile to the soul? So he crafted a retreat using raw and evocative songs—and a few principles of group dynamics.

He began his first experiment, a forty-eight-hour retreat, by collecting watches and radios and gathering a group of suspicious sailors in a circle. To their relief, he explained that he would not be doing any teaching or preaching. He said he had prepared some music just for them. "All that I'm going to do," he explained, "is push *play*, push *stop*, and listen to anything you want to say. What you do with this is up to you."

Harris turned on the cassette and unleashed a torrent of rock, blues, and poetry, each line stained by anguish and punctuated with an earthy honesty that could make a Marine blush. Janis Joplin, Leonard Cohen, Tom Waits, Johnny Cash, and a choir of lesser-knowns bellowed out ballads about what it feels like to be abused, scorned, yelled at by parents, abandoned, drunk, drugged, and raped.

The initial blocks of music were loosely bound together by painful emotional themes. The last two collections were created to infuse hope and point to the transforming love of God. And, according to Don, for the majority of those collected in that first circle, it worked. Razor-sharp honesty and pulsating bass chiseled through hardened hearts and opened passages for grace to seep in. Perhaps Leonard Cohen summarized it best when he sang that Sunday morning: "There is a crack in everything. That's how the light get's in." [1]

I discovered Donald Harris after he had retired from the Navy. His program became known as "Credo," and at its peak of popularity, twelve chaplains were employed to lead Credo groups around the world.

After hearing about his creative approach to soul healing, I tracked him down because I wanted to invite him to take a group of counselors in training through a civilian version of Credo. The retreat would be part of a class on the personal and spiritual lives of therapists.

He graciously agreed, traveled to our campus, and uncorked his musical elixir for twenty or so Christian counselors, most of whom had neither been in uniform nor experienced the subterranean layers of pain so graphically described in those lyrics. Some were shocked; some were put off, offended, but the majority had an experience very similar to that of the sailors. Those confessed that listening to the soulful admissions of brokenness and pain created feelings of deep empathy and dialogue. They quit hiding the thin cracks in their souls, which was precisely where the Light began to pour in . . . and then back out.

Reflection

Using the Brokenness

Over the years I've heard many success stories from Chaplain Harris's approach to dealing with pain as part of the process of transformation. In fact, it has transformed the way I tend to look at brokenness and suffering. On a personal level, when I experience emotional pain—be it rejection, loneliness, grief, depression, or fear—I begin to look for and to celebrate these "cracks," to pray that through them, because of them, God's light will come pouring in. And when it does, I become a little freer from the illusion that it is possible to thrive separate from the power and energy of God. I believe that apprentices to Jesus are learning to work in and with the light that comes pouring through the brokenness in their lives.

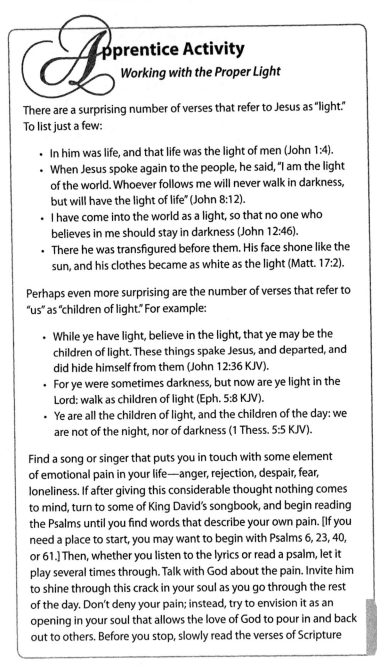

pprentice Activity

Working with the Proper Light

There are a surprising number of verses that refer to Jesus as "light."
To list just a few:

- In him was life, and that life was the light of men (John 1:4).
- When Jesus spoke again to the people, he said, "I am the light of the world. Whoever follows me will never walk in darkness, but will have the light of life" (John 8:12).
- I have come into the world as a light, so that no one who believes in me should stay in darkness (John 12:46).
- There he was transfigured before them. His face shone like the sun, and his clothes became as white as the light (Matt. 17:2).

Perhaps even more surprising are the number of verses that refer to "us" as "children of light." For example:

- While ye have light, believe in the light, that ye may be the children of light. These things spake Jesus, and departed, and did hide himself from them (John 12:36 KJV).
- For ye were sometimes darkness, but now are ye light in the Lord: walk as children of light (Eph. 5:8 KJV).
- Ye are all the children of light, and the children of the day: we are not of the night, nor of darkness (1 Thess. 5:5 KJV).

Find a song or singer that puts you in touch with some element of emotional pain in your life—anger, rejection, despair, fear, loneliness. If after giving this considerable thought nothing comes to mind, turn to some of King David's songbook, and begin reading the Psalms until you find words that describe your own pain. [If you need a place to start, you may want to begin with Psalms 6, 23, 40, or 61.] Then, whether you listen to the lyrics or read a psalm, let it play several times through. Talk with God about the pain. Invite him to shine through this crack in your soul as you go through the rest of the day. Don't deny your pain; instead, try to envision it as an opening in your soul that allows the love of God to pour in and back out to others. Before you stop, slowly read the verses of Scripture listed above and then make Ephesians 5:8b–10 your prayer for the day:

- Live as children of light (for the fruit of the light consists in all goodness, righteousness and truth) and find out what pleases the Lord.

Then go through the rest of the day, allowing yourself to be totally alive and available to each present moment. And in each moment ask Christ to move through you in ways that are most pleasing to him.

Simmering in Colossians 3:1–17 Continued. Please slowly reread verses 1–11 and then meditatively ponder verse 12:

As God's chosen ones, holy and beloved, clothe yourselves with compassion, kindness, humility, meekness, and patience.

27

The Need to Slow Down

Hurry Is the Devil

Hurry is not of the devil; hurry is the devil.

—Carl Jung

After eight days on the road, the plane touched down thirty minutes ahead of schedule. The stewardess made sure that fact had not escaped our notice with a light-hearted PA announcement. But as a seasoned traveler I knew what an early arrival meant—extra time on the tarmac while waiting for the plane at our arrival gate to push back. No problem, I had another chapter to read.

Forty minutes later, we finally deplaned and I bolted for the underground train. When I arrived at baggage claim, I saw my wife. We hugged in a way that would have embarrassed our children, but eight days was way too long to be away.

After disentangling and then catching up for a while, it occurred to me that we'd been waiting for my one piece of checked luggage for a long time. I glanced at a clock. Forty-five minutes had passed. I began to consider whether I really needed the items in the bag and how St. Francis might handle the situation, as a fellow passenger was returning from inquiring at the baggage counter.

He laughed as he relayed the response he got. "The guy said, 'Have you been waiting for at least an hour?' When I replied, 'No, just forty-five minutes,' he said not to come back until it had been at least an hour."

"Hmmm," I said, "anybody that's paying $150.00 for a checked bag should consider buying it a seat on the plane. At least you wouldn't have to wait, and you could eat its peanuts."

The luggage finally arrived right on time—one hour late.

We got into the car just after 11 p.m. It would be a 110-mile drive and I didn't want to do the math on when I'd be reunited with my own bed. When I saw that one of the pay-for-parking exit lanes was shorter, I went for it so fast we almost got whiplash. But it was worth it. There was only one car in front of us.

Ten minutes later the same car was still blocking the way to my bed. I couldn't see the face of the driver of the minivan, but the person had been engaged in a long and animated conversation with the attendant. Two cars had already exited my lane for longer but faster exit options. The conversation continued, so I did the only polite thing I could think of, I flashed my high-beams. No effect—other than my wife's disapproving groan.

Another five minutes passed; another flash, another groan.

By this point all the other lanes had filled and emptied at least three times over. But now they were all full again and there was still only one car in front of me, a minivan apparently piloted by the parking attendant's long lost friend from elementary school with years of catching up to do.

Finally the gate swung up. But what's this! The conversation continued. I glanced at my wife. She was not looking. I gave in to the urge that had been building for over fifteen minutes and blew the horn. A mighty blast, loud and long. The driver of the van stuck her entire torso out and shouted back at me, "So what's your problem!" before finally driving away.

I assumed it was a rhetorical question and that she would discover the answer in her mirror, so I didn't respond. I pulled up to the window and immediately began to explain, "Look, I'm sorry about that, but after forty minutes on the tarmac, an hour waiting for baggage, twenty minutes in this lane, I just ran out of patience."

The attendant was nice but ignored my sin offering and explained, "That lady there has a van full of kids. One of them got sick on the plane and they had to call an ambulance to meet them in the parking structure. With all the distractions, she lost her ticket and I was trying to work it out so she wouldn't have to pay for parking on top of the $400 ambulance bill. She's headed to the emergency room right now."

Oh, great. I had just returned from eight days of telling people about what it means to be like Jesus, and in the midst of my impatience I blasted my horn at a distraught mother, four little children, and the parking attendant who was actually *being* like Jesus. The only saving grace was that my wife was kind enough to avoid stating the obvious.

As I pulled out onto the highway, I began to ponder why it is that I feel such an inner urge to race off to the future when I know one of the fundamental spiritual facts of the universe: all of life happens in the present moment. What is the root of this compulsion and what does it cost?

Driving north, I remembered a scene from the movie *Smoke* that makes a powerful point about the need to slow down and be present if we are to notice the really important stuff in life.

By the time we get to that point in the film, we have already met Auggie Wren (Harvey Keitel), owner of a tobacco shop that serves as a backdrop for conversations among the locals. The discussions at Auggie's are philosophical, like Sir Walter Raleigh's wager that he could measure the weight of smoke and subsequent comparisons of smoke to the soul.

Anyway, Auggie develops a conversational relationship with the novelist Paul Benjamin (William Hurt), who is still recovering from the death of his wife three years before. She was killed by a stray bullet just moments after leaving Auggie's shop where she had stopped to buy Paul some cigars.

One evening Auggie shows Paul his "Life Work," over 4,000 pictures of the same thing—the corner of 3rd Street and 7th Avenue. Each frame is taken at 8 a.m. each morning, rain or shine, blizzard or heat wave. Paul seems appreciative of the effort but begins flipping through the pages very quickly after he realizes the sameness of each shot, saying, "I don't get it." That is when Auggie offers: "You'll never get it if you don't slow down, my friend. You're going too fast, hardly even looking at the pictures. They are all the same, but each one is different from every other one. It's just one place in the world, but things take place there like everywhere else: bright mornings and dreary mornings, autumn light and summer light, weekdays and weekends. How people are dressed. How many times it's the same person in the shot. Each day the earth revolves around the sun, and every day the light hits the earth at a different angle."

Paul slows down and carefully studies the differences in each frame. It's not long until he sees something that causes him to sob with joy. His wife, Ellen, is in several of the photos. He's able for a few seconds to step into the photos, to be with her on the sidewalk again. And he would have missed it if he'd continued to flip through the pages as unobserved present moments—like so many of us, desperately in a hurry to race off to the future when the best parts of life are found only by slowing down to fully experience the present.

I glanced at my wife who is studying the Atlanta skyline, and I wondered how many present moments I had lost just in the past two hours.

Reflection

Jesus Was Never in a Hurry

I squeezed my wife's hand and smiled. But before I could settle into the present, my mind was off again in a flash; this time to the past. I recalled being in a class with Dallas Willard up in the San Gabriel Mountains above Sierra Madre. There were about thirty of us in the class anticipating the special experience— Dallas's teaching in a beautiful retreat center setting. Could there be a better occasion for academic or spiritual insights?

My mind went back to the first thing that came out of his mouth—after he had led the class in singing a few hymns, adjusted his notes, and settled in behind the podium.

"I want each of you to go away from this place and never hurry again. Hurry is always an expression of anxiety and the sign of a deeper problem."

And in case we were looking to ministry as a loophole, he underlined his hope for us. "And remember: 'One of the greatest enemies to service to Jesus is service to Jesus.' If you are not experiencing your yoke as easy and your burden as light, then you are bearing some other burden, but not the burden of Christ—it is a problem with your heart."[1]

That night in a small cell of a retreat room I wrote about the challenge in my journal. I knew what the problem was for me. I don't feel fully confident in my sense of worth to God and others. I don't feel confident that I am loved by God. As a result, I often take on projects to feel better about myself, to make a name for myself, to have some sense of accomplishment. And then as the commitments mount and the deadlines approach, I begin to buckle under the weight of the obligations. And by this point, I feel that I'm in it alone. I'm not doing this "with God" anymore. And it's become too much to do by myself.

Meanwhile, because the day-timer has become so full, I often begin to ignore the most important things in life, like being a good husband, father, son, brother, and friend. By this point in my maelstrom of anxiety-driven hurry, the attention I give to friends and family is often out of obligation. My plans for being a good provider are ofen self-serving—allowing me to limit my obligations. That is, telling myself I need to hurry up and put some more money in the bank—for the college or wedding fund—so I can get back to my checklists. I see it. I know the ugly truth of it. It's a circle of anxiety and hurry.

And then there's Jesus. He was never in a hurry. He waited four millennia to show up in the flesh. He spent his first thirty years pursuing a dead-end job as a carpenter, and then he spent the next three years—his entire career—camping out with his friends. He even showed up two days late when one of his best friends, Lazarus, died. Jesus was never in a hurry. What was his secret? I think it has to do with identity and power.

In the months that have followed my late-night reminder to slow down and be more fully available to the present moment, I've discovered that two reflections—from Dallas's writings, of course—have helped me tremendously. When I recall my truest identity as a "never ceasing spiritual being," it helps me to realize that I have far more time than I can even imagine. And when I meditate on both the power and presence of God, I often gain a tremendous sense of being yoked to a nuclear power plant—but in a good way. That is, I'm learning to face each day from the perspective of being in an apprenticeship with God.

This all sounds pretty flowery, but last week this new approach was put to the test. The opening scene once again was at Hartsfield airport. My wife, Regina, was dropping me off, and in spite of all the improvement, I was coming down with another case of hurry sickness. I left her that morning feeling very confused and stressed. I felt that I had to give up at least two major projects, and picking the ones to let go had begun to feel like *Sophie's Choice*. As I waved goodbye one last time from the curb, I muttered a prayer to God about needing to feel more of a sense that he still remembered who I was and was willing to work with me, side by side.

Then it started. A once-every-three-years-or-so upgrade to first class caused me to wonder if it were a wink from God. It certainly resulted in a more quiet three hours for conversation with him. The next three days were sprinkled with affirmations—calls from friends to say they appreciated that I was on the planet, a chance meeting with someone who had read one of my books and was composing a letter to say thank you, a couple of gifts targeted to exact needs, and so on. And then it really started, four different people approached me and offered their help and expertise as a writer, editor, or administrator. And then with almost no effort on my part, a dream team of people emerged who were willing to work with me on a project of mutual interest. Before I returned home, my appreciation of the easy yoke of Christ had reached new heights as had my enthusiasm for the gift of being a "never ceasing spiritual being" in a hilarious interactive friendship with God.

So I did the only sensible thing. I slowed down and smelled a few roses.

pprentice Activity
Sleep, Play, Then Work

Each week contains the same amount of hours—168 of them. If you divide that by three, you realize that you have equal amounts of time for three very important things: *sleep* (56 hours, or an average of 8 hours per night); *work* (you certainly can work less, but this amount will let workaholics or those with a long commute in on this); and *play/recreation* (yep, 56 marvelous hours each week for play, relaxation, exercise, etc.).

Map out an ideal schedule for yourself. From the preceding math that's been done for you, note that you can block out 112 hours for sleep and recreation. You are encouraged to only allow yourself to work half that amount of time. With the big blocks in place, fill in the gaps. But here are some suggestions:

- Schedule *sleep* first.
- Add *play/recreation* to each day—and don't forget to put in time for exercise, friends, and family, and wasting time with God.
- Schedule *work* last—up to 56 hours—but keep a Sabbath if at all possible.

Simmering in Colossians 3:1–17 Continued. Please slowly reread verses 1–12 and then meditatively ponder verse 13:

Bear with one another and, if anyone has a complaint against another, forgive each other; just as the Lord has forgiven you, so you also must forgive.

Eating a Balanced Diet

The Six Streams of Christian Spirituality

Today a mighty river of the Spirit is bursting forth from the hearts of women and men, boys and girls. It is a deep river of divine intimacy, a powerful river of holy living, a dancing river of jubilation in the Spirit, and a broad river of unconditional love for all peoples. As Jesus says, "Out of the believers' heart shall flow rivers of living water."

—Richard J. Foster

The restaurant is an amazing invention. You walk in and a total stranger says, "Hello," like you were old friends, and escorts you to a table. Then, before you can settle in, another nice person drops a napkin in your lap and offers to bring you stuff to eat. As much as you want!

Shortly, he returns with a steaming plate of food. Then, after you finish committing various acts of gluttony, you get up, walk out, and leave someone else with the mess to clean up. And before you can get through the door, several smiling faces suggest that you have a wonderful day. Wow! No wonder this concept has caught on.

Can you imagine the first time someone thought of that concept? Perhaps Abel said to his wife, "Honey, I don't feel much like hunting today, and you look a bit frazzled from all the hide tanning. Why don't we go on over to Cain's house and ask them to cook us up a mess of vegetables, smile at us while we eat, and then clean it up while telling us to have a good day?"

It's not surprising that the first attempt at going out to eat had a tragic ending. But with time, the concept became refined.

Years ago it occurred to me that eating out is also a great way to save money. Lots of it! Suppose you'd like to take your spouse to Paris but don't have three days or $2,500 lying around. No problem. Just go out for a lunch at a fancy French restaurant and *voilà*! There you are. Paris, complete with a snooty waiter who makes fun of you when you try to order their famous fries, water with bubbles, and enough bread to fill a half-starved dog. And you saved about $2,450 in the process.

The same plan works for going to China, India, Lebanon, Germany, Cuba, Mexico, and England. I don't like to brag, but last year alone my family saved close to $500,000 in travel costs by eating out.

Speaking of eating out, I witnessed something unusual a couple of weeks ago when I was visiting Thailand—if you know what I mean—on a business lunch. Unbeknownst to me, one of our eating companions had some severe food allergies. Just before he was about to order, one of his colleagues nudged me and said, "Listen, you won't believe what you are about to hear."

And I didn't. It sounded something like this.

"Uh, excuse me," he said to the "tour guide." "I can't have any spices in my food."

The waiter nodded, while likely wondering why his customer had wandered into a Thai restaurant.

"I mean *any* spices. And I can't have sauces either—brown, white, soy, duck, or goose."

Another nod.

"If I have any MSG, I'll break out in hives. Same for all the glutamates. And no nitro-sodium syntax, or mono-neucleo-digestital. No B-12s, B-3s or B-52s."

At that, someone in the back yelled "Bingo."

He wasn't finished. "And how is your rice cooked?"

"Huh?"

"Because I can't have anything come in contact with my rice but distilled water and sea salt."

At this point, the waiter left while the man continued to describe what he could not eat—lest he swell to the size of Marlon Brando in *Superman*. The owner appeared and stood behind the patron as he continued. He too was taking notes. That's right. One customer, two people taking notes—three if you count me; I knew I'd be using this someday.

". . . and I can't eat any animals or their by-products."

Just the thought of an animal's by-product was about to make me swell up, myself.

". . . and how the pan is prepared is very important. No fats of any kind, from whale blubber to canola oil . . . and no vegetables that are iron rich, or my eyes will bulge out to here . . . and . . ."

After about five more minutes of this, he was finished. The patient owner nodded, turned, and walked away—no doubt to reconsider the insurance business as an alternative line of work.

"Is there anything you *can* eat besides poached manna?" I asked.

No response.

In a few minutes, a waiter returned with his order. Carrots and snow peas in a Pepto-Bismol sauce, resting on a bed of rice, gently steamed in distilled water. It was the worst trip to Thailand I had ever witnessed.

Reflection

Avoiding an Eating Disorder

Food allergies are not fun and I don't mean to make fun of my friend, but I do mean to use the experience to make a point. For years of my life I approached the concept of drawing sustenance from other Christian traditions with the same level of pickiness.

Renovaré, a ministry dedicated to helping people become more like Jesus, has been greatly inspired by the life-work of both Richard J. Foster and Dallas Willard. In addition to promoting a practical strategy for spiritual formation—through engagement with the classic spiritual disciplines and classic devotional literature—Renovaré also promotes a balanced approach. That is, they offer the assertion that Jesus is the source of each of the great traditions of Christian spirituality—Contemplative (prayer-filled life), Holiness (virtuous life), Charismatic (Spirit-empowered life), Social Justice (compassionate life), Evangelical (Word-centered life), and Incarnational (sacramental life). They also suggest that it is a healthy thing to be nourished by each of these wonderful expressions. An overarching characteristic of each of these traditions is presented below:

Contemplative	Spending time with God in prayer and meditation.
Holiness	Having an identity "in Christ," which leads to pure thoughts, words, and actions, and overcoming temptation.
Charismatic	Welcoming the Holy Spirit while nurturing and exercising spiritual gifts.
Social Justice	Helping others less fortunate than I.
Evangelical	Studying the Scriptures and sharing the gospel of Jesus Christ—especially as a living witness of transformation.
Incarnational	Unifying the sacred and secular areas of my life while experiencing and showing God's presence.

Richard J. Foster beautifully writes about each of these traditions in *Streams of Living Water: Celebrating the Great Traditions of Christian Faith*. He refers to each as a "stream" that can trace its source to the heart of Christ. It's a wonderfully appropriate metaphor.

When I talk about the need for a balanced approach to Christian spiritual formation, I like to consider each of the great traditions as being analogous to the six major food groups: grains, vegetables, fruits, dairy, meats, oils/fats. While it pales by comparison to the "streams" metaphor, it does make an important point. As with our physical diets, it is very healthy to consume from each of the food groups. In fact, picky eating patterns or consuming from only one food group—even if it's vegetables (which I use as a symbol for Holiness offerings)—can lead to a spiritual eating disorder. I won't complete my comparison list of traditions and food groups for fear of unintentionally offending with my caricatures. I especially don't want to offend my Charismatic (oils for anointing) or Social Justice (fruit for getting the bowels of compassion moving) friends. Oops.

The point to all this is simple. The diet of an apprentice is very important. We need to eat what Jesus ate—we need to draw nourishment from each of the six major spiritual food groups.

pprentice Activity
Eating a Balanced Diet

Take a few minutes to consider the six streams/food groups described above and then provide a ruthlessly honest evaluation of where you are with each. In the image below, you will find the Streams arranged in a table. Take a few moments and, using a scale of 1 to 5 (with 1 being the least proficient—for you), estimate where you are in each of these six areas. Circle the number in each column that best expresses where you are.

Contemplative: Spending time with God in prayer and meditation.	1	2	3	4	5
Holiness: Having pure thoughts, words, and actions, and overcoming temptation.	1	2	3	4	5
Charismatic: Welcoming the Holy Spirit while nurturing and exercising my spiritual gifts.	1	2	3	4	5
Social Justice: Helping others less fortunate than I.	1	2	3	4	5
Evangelical: Sharing the gospel of Jesus Christ and reading the Scriptures.	1	2	3	4	5
Incarnational: Unifying the sacred and secular areas of my life while showing forth God's presence.	1	2	3	4	5

Now, as part of having a "more balanced diet," from the list below choose exercises that correspond to your two lowest scores and participate in the suggested practice.

Stream /"Food Group" Exercise

- *Contemplative*: The prayer-filled life emphasizes loving God. As St. Augustine has said, "True, whole prayer is nothing but love." Take 10 to 15 minutes to compose a prayer to God in which you communicate only your love for him—no requests, favors, or details from your life—nothing but your love for him. Then take some time to listen to his reply.[1]
- *Holiness*: Colossians 3:1–17 offers a beautiful listing of "rules for holy living." If you have not been memorizing this passage, take a moment to read it through—slowly. Ask God to prompt you with how this passage can encourage holy living—this very day.
- *Charismatic*: Watch the movie *The Princess Bride* with your family—or by yourself. Then, for the next twenty-four hours, see how many times you can express your love for God by saying, "As you wish."[2]
- *Social Justice*: Meditate on James 1:27: *"Religion that is pure and undefiled before God, the Father, is this: to care for orphans*

and widows in their distress, and to keep oneself unstained by the world" (NRSV). Ask God what this verse means for you and your walk with him; then ask how you can practice a pure and undefiled religion this week.[3]

- *Evangelical:* You are likely familiar with St. Francis's famous quote, "Preach every day, and if necessary, use words." This week preach at least one wordless sermon about the love of God.[4]

- *Incarnational:* Make a "game" out of your work tomorrow. Offer everything you do in your vocation as a gift to God. Let each action be offered up as an act of service—whether you are preparing food for hungry children, mopping a floor, changing a transmission, or balancing a spreadsheet. Perhaps you will want to punctuate your work with a breathed prayer, such as, "I'm doing this work *with* you and *for you.*"[5]

Simmering in Colossians 3:1–17 Continued. Please slowly reread verses 1–13 and then meditatively ponder verse 14:

Above all, clothe yourselves with love, which binds everything together in perfect harmony.

Becoming a Master Craftsman

It's All about the VIM and Vigor

What we have been told is how we can be drawn into Christ—can become part of that wonderful present which the young Prince of the universe wants to offer to His Father—that present which is Himself and therefore us in Him. It is the only thing we were made for.

—C. S. Lewis[1]

I have a great desire to speak a foreign language fluently—any foreign language. I've made at least four attempts. In high school I took French for two years; I was even president of the French club. What a disaster, trying to learn how to speak a soft, flowing language in the rural south—even our teacher *parlez vous*-ed with a drawl. Whenever I tried to speak, I felt like I was ordering Chateaubriand at a Waffle House. My only comfort was in the hope I held that if I ever traveled in Europe the locals might assume I was from the South of France.

Actually I did travel in a French-speaking part of the world. I found myself lost one evening in the city of Geneva. When I looked around and realized I could no longer see the location marker I had been using—the giant fountain spraying up from Lake Geneva—I panicked and began asking everyone I met if they knew where my hotel was located. As it turns out, I was telling them that I had lost my blue pencil box and then asking if they could help me by pointing to the giant spout of pee that was soaking their beautiful city. After several minutes of this, a kind lady asked me in perfect English if I needed any help. Before I could exclaim "Oui!" she pointed me in the right direction.

Three decades have passed and my French vocabulary has eroded to three words, *oui* and *très peu*—which ironically means "yes, very little."

I studied Hebrew for two years in college, and for the time it took to take one final exam, I could let a Hebrew Bible flop open to any section and read a chapter or so. I did the same thing with Greek in seminary. But now, I know exactly three times as much French as I do Hebrew and Greek.

My last attempt at language learning was Russian. As someone who lived through the Cold War, had friends with bomb shelters, and then later came to realize that Moscow was once considered the "third Rome," and that Orthodox theology was as refreshing as drinking from the headwaters of a stream, I became fascinated with the country and set out to learn the language.

I'm thinking about this because, as I was rolling out of bed this morning, a book caught my eye. It was on the bottom shelf of a fern table that doubles as a lamp stand. I bought it years ago because the title promised that I would *Learn Russian in Ten Minutes a Day*. That book is a liar.

Ten years later, after taking the book up on its offer by plowing through its pages, filling our house with stick-on labels, and hiring a tutor from St. Petersburg for a few sessions, I can't order a кофеий (coffee) in a кафе (café) or count the монетки (coins) in my change. After an initial burst of energy and excitement, I gave up. For the fourth time I gave up on language learning. The book came to its final resting place where it has collected dust for the better part of a decade.

The truth is that while I thought it would be fun to speak and read Russian (and French, and Hebrew, and Greek), I had no sustaining *vision*—I could never really imagine Russian words flying out of my mouth or leaping off the page. Nor did I have the requisite *intention*, the white-knuckled determination to pay the price required for learning a new language. And while I had some *means* available—like that book and even a Russian tutor for a few weeks—I did not immerse myself in those methods and resources. I lacked both the VIM[2] (vision, intention, and means) and the vigor for real change. That was unfortunate. Dallas Willard believes that if a person learns any new thing—including becoming more like Jesus—it will be by way of the VIM model.

Vision

Learning a new language requires a sustainable vision that this is possible. The vision will need to be fueled by holding before the mind all of the advantages of being able to speak and write in a new language. I'm sure it is easier to hold on to such a vision if you live in the middle of Switzerland where a leisurely Sunday drive in any direction will have you in the midst of at least four different cultures. And I would assume that visions for language learning are more difficult to come by for someone immersed in the heart of a mono-lingual country—but meeting a soul mate who happens to be a foreign exchange student could help.

For a person to work the steps of AA successfully, he must begin with a vision of how life can be different—a life of sobriety. Sometimes seeing the negative impact of drinking on the lives of a spouse or children can help bring the need for sobriety into focus. But for the program of change to have a chance to work, a person beginning to work the 12 Steps must be able to see himself free from addiction.

In the imagery of Christian transformation, *vision* refers to the ability to see ourselves radically transformed and authentically living life a whole new way in God's kingdom on earth—head-over-heels in love with both Creator and his creation. A person with a vision for transformation sees the *journey of salvation*, the imagery of the *Trinity*, and the *kingdom of heaven* with new eyes. God's offer is much more than a "get out of hell free" card; he is inviting us to become his apprentice and friend, being *with* him until we are like him.

When I read where Jesus says to love my neighbor as much as I love myself, could he have really meant that? Do I have the eyes to actually see myself doing that? Can I imagine actually turning the unbruised cheek to someone who has hit me?

It has been my intention in writing this book to offer stories that might help create a new vision for the possibility of life with God as an intimate, transforming friendship.

Intention

Learning a new language also requires motivation. I went much further in my Hebrew and Greek learning than for either French or Russian because I was more motivated. For starters, I knew that I would need a passable knowledge of Hebrew and Greek to graduate from seminary. The desire to read Scripture in the original languages also fueled my intention for mastery. And for both of these languages—for at least a little while—the goal was achieved. What I lacked was the sustaining intention to spend the necessary time each day to keep those languages alive. As the intention waned, so did the ability to parse verbs; it took a bit longer for me to forget how to split infinitives.

When it comes to sobriety, the vision of a new way to live makes it possible for us to intend to live life in a radically different manner. An alcoholic has never stopped drinking without forming the ironclad intention to do so.

In the context of Christian transformation, a person must intend to live in the kingdom of God by willing to obey the precise example and teachings of Jesus. If we are to get on with the process of authentic transformation, we must intend to pick up our cross and follow Christ with a resolve to continue no matter what internal and external obstacles may block the path. And we must act on those intentions.

The two most important images from the life of Christ are the cross and the empty tomb. The two most important decisions an apprentice of Jesus can make are to accept our own personal cross—the place where self-will is crucified—and to embrace the mystery of Paul's words, "I no longer live, but Christ lives in me" (Gal. 2:20).

An apprentice of Christ must *will* to have no other will than the will of God and be willing to endure the crucifixion of self-determination. "Oh, God," I cry, "there must be some other way. Surely you cannot expect me to approach you the same way those AA members approach their meetings?" There is no other way that leads to authentic transformation.

When I read survey after survey showing minimal differences between Christians and non-Christians, the first three questions that fire in my head are: Were these Christians given a sustainable vision for a radically different way to live? Were they taught the foundational importance of becoming settled in having an unwavering intention to change? Were they presented with time-tested methods, or means, for transformation?

Means

Vision and intention are like insight and motivation in psychotherapy—they are the necessary but often insufficient elements of change. There must also be a path, or the means to change. In language learning the means is the curriculum or course of study. Arguably there are no better means for language learning than total immersion in the life, language, and culture that is being studied.

The tried-and-true means to sobriety are the 12 Steps of AA (against the backdrop of community support). Honesty (including confession), surrender, and community are the proven means of AA programs around the world.

Even with both vision and intention, transformation also requires the *means* for change—activities of being with and learning from. But for many, these "spiritual disciplines" can become pointless acts of drudgery instead of creative ways of enjoying the presence of another. If so, it is likely we'll abandon both the means and the master because of the mundane methodology.

In a serious program for Christian formation, the means for transformation include: openness to the presence and power of Christ, study of his life and teachings, inspiration from seekers and saints, and the practice of classic Christian disciplines. These are the means to change for a person with the vision for and intention to change. And also like the AA program, it can take a lot of pain—the repeated realizations that we are not equipped to run our lives without help from the designer—to bring a person to readiness to enter into an apprenticeship with Jesus.

An apprentice to Christ is someone who is determined to be with him, in a posture of openness and receptivity, for the purpose of becoming what he is. It's a tall task. In fact, it's an impossible task—unless we realize the secret of the easy yoke, allowing Jesus to live his life through us as we go through each moment of the day *with* him as our guide, teacher, and animator of the life we want to live.

Reflection
What It Takes to Change

This book is written to present a model for entering into an apprenticeship with Jesus. I purposely used the word *apprenticeship* instead of *discipleship* to imply learning through co-laboring with and experiential awareness of the real presence of Christ. There is nothing wrong with the word *discipleship*, but I believe time has weathered it with the unwanted implications of *learning facts about* a historic figure instead of *working with* a present friend.

My fondest hope is that, in getting to this page, you will have found a new vision for yourself—as an unceasing spiritual being—and for God as a creative and compassionate community of three who has invited you to join their dance. This new vision is perhaps best captured by the old words of the Baltimore Catechism: "Why did God make me? . . . God made me to know him, to love him, and to serve him and to be happy with him forever."

I also hope that such a vision will fuel a deep and unshakable intention to learn from him, living each moment of our day by his side as an apprentice, and that perhaps some of the apprentice activities have become a means of transformation.

pprentice Activity

Maintaining the VIM and Vigor for Your Apprenticeship

Take a moment to write down your personal VIM model for transformation. What is your *vision*? How would you describe your level of *intention* for staying with an apprentice program? What are the most effective *means* for transformation that you have experienced?

A Personal VIM Statement

VISION:

_____
_____
_____
_____
_____

INTENTION:

_____
_____
_____
_____
_____

MEANS:

_____
_____
_____
_____

Simmering in Colossians 3:1–17 Continued. Please slowly reread verses 1–14 and then meditatively ponder verse 15:

And let the peace of Christ rule in your hearts, to which indeed you were called in the one body. And be thankful.

30

DAY

The Best Way to Apprentice Others

Live the Transformation You Want to See in Them

Acquire inward peace, and thousands around you will find their salvation.

—St. Seraphim of Sarov

Norman had cow eyes. Big. Round. Brown. Innocent. They were the first things I noticed when he appeared out of nowhere.

He claimed to be twelve, but he looked more like a thin ten. His faded blue jeans were peppered with holes and looked about three sizes too big. In America he'd have been "styling." But this wasn't LA. It was city-center San Jose, Costa Rica. Norman just looked poor.

Norman had a million-dollar smile, though. It was more than enough to buy the attention of everyone in our group.

The group? There were about twenty of us—huddled together under a canvas awning in the front of a little shop trying to stay dry. We'd been waiting for about an hour for a late-afternoon rainstorm to finish washing the bricks of the plaza where the youth of our "mission team" would be performing. In the meantime, the attention of the group was focused on Norman. He soaked it up like a dry sponge.

We talked with him, sort of. Collectively we had the Spanish skills of an eighteen-month-old child. But it was enough. We learned Norman's age. Found out where he lived. That he no longer went to school, worked twelve hours a day to support his family, and had a smile that could melt ice.

The rain slowed. The drama troupe raced to the center of the two-acre stone plaza and began to perform. Norman followed. He stood in the drizzle and watched three performances. At the end of the third performance a small group of the kids talked with Norman and in broken Spanish led him in repeating the "sinner's prayer." My daughter then gave him her Spanish-English Bible. Norman's face lit up like it was Christmas morning. He clutched it tenderly and brushed it against his chin.

Norman was invited to accompany our youth group to where they would be performing again. He didn't have to be asked twice. Halfway to the second locale someone in our group needed to visit a restroom. We stopped at a no-name fast-food restaurant. Norman was still the center of the conversation.

Carlos, an older local who had joined us, asked me what part of the city Norman was from. I had forgotten what Norman had told us, so I asked Carlos to ask him directly. A cloud of shame passed across Norman's eyes when he told the man—who knew the city—where he was from. Pity formed in Carlos's eyes.

"Where is he from?" I whispered to Carlos.

"Oh," Carlos said, "it's the worst part of town. The people there go through garbage to find something to eat."

I looked down at Norman. I'd never seen that kind of poverty before, face-to-face.

Without thinking, I took him by the hand to the food counter. Talking with my hands, I invited Norman to buy anything on the menu, then everything on the menu.

Norman ordered in Spanish. His request arrived: one small, quarter-cup, carton of ice cream.

"No!" I gestured. "Order more. Order everything!"

I pointed to the picture that contained the most food and said "He'll have two of those."

The person at the counter seemed to understand. The order came in a large bag. We found a table, but something strange happened. Norman wouldn't eat. He seemed very content, but only sipped his drink, clutched the bag of food, and smiled. With some coaxing he did finish his ice cream, but try as we might, he would not open the bag.

Our group had already gone, so I eventually stood and led Norman out of the restaurant with an arm around his back. We arrived at the second site for the performance. For more than an hour Norman laughed and smiled, tapped girls on the shoulder and ran, caught raindrops on his tongue and watched our drama team. And he clutched his bag of food.

Eventually, we had to leave. Norman walked us to where our vans were parked. He passed out hugs to the women and stiff-back handshakes to the men. After letting go of my hand, he took off into the night. He darted through an ocean of city traffic as skillful as a squirrel on tree limbs. A light rain was still falling. He held his bag of food close to his chest and disappeared into the night.

And it was at about that moment the answer to the mystery finally popped into my head. I knew why a hungry boy wouldn't eat. Norman was taking the food home to his family.

I was awash with alternating waves of deep joy and shame. Norman was the missionary. His sermon was one of the most powerful I had ever heard. That little boy's life of desperate poverty had become a furnace burning away the dross of self-ishness. I don't think there was much left inside but gold.

I have no doubt I'll see Norman again. I just hope when we meet in heaven he won't be ashamed to visit me on the "poor side of town."

Those few hours with Norman took place years ago, but I've found myself revisiting them often. I like to think that as he shared his food with his family he also shared images from the drama he saw. I like to think that he spent time flipping through the Bible he was given that night and that on many occasions he heard the voice of the Holy Spirit prompting him to read, explaining the difficult passages.

Other times I question the value of what happened that night—other than the ministry we received from Norman. Should we have used the money to feed thirty families like Norman's for a year? Is there kingdom value in a "magic phrase" approach to evangelism—giving the "right" answer to a question about Jesus—when there is no follow-up for apprentice making?

Don't get me wrong. I'm a big fan of both Billy Graham and his crusades. But a big part of his wisdom involves mobilizing local churches and an army of volunteers to do follow-up and to offer options for discipleship training. I know that. I see the value. But even when the efforts are more organized and ongoing, the question that launched this book remains. Why is there so little evidence that those of us who use the term "Christian" as part of our self-identification show so little difference from those who do not? Maybe it's time to consider a new approach and a special kiss.

A Special Kiss

Milton Hershey—the man who first envisioned a chocolate kiss—was born in Pennsylvania in 1857 to Mennonite parents. He was raised on a farm and stopped going to school after the fourth grade. At the age of eighteen Milton Hershey turned in his farm clothes and became an apprentice to a chocolate maker. After a period of learning the craft, and a few false starts, Milton became a very successful candy man.

He founded the Lancaster Caramel Corporation and in time sold it for one million dollars—a huge sum for the mid-1800s. But his heart was not in caramel; it was in chocolate. So Milton invested his fortune into a chocolate factory and the research of chocolate. Milton Hershey had a simple idea. He wanted to make the world's best-tasting chocolate—with no apologies to the Swiss.

At the conclusion of his experiments in chocolate making, he built a plant in Hershey, Pennsylvania. The green dairy land was a logical choice, since he needed to be close to a dependable supply of fresh milk for the production of milk chocolate. Until that time, milk chocolate had been a luxury item primarily known in parts of Europe.

Hershey's product was an immediate success, and he poured much of the profits into philanthropic projects and the building of a model town for his workers.

But these factors are not why I'm telling this story. Milton Hershey didn't believe in "advertising." In fact, until the early 1970s the Hershey Corporation did not put a dime into advertising. The philosophy of the founder was simply this: if you make the world's best chocolate, word will get out. No need to advertise if you really are producing something that everyone craves.

When it comes to advertising and product development, Hershey used the same approach as Jesus. Christ's focus was on product development too: produce people whose hearts truly are renovated—bursting with love, peace, joy, humility, truth, and power—and the world will want in. Jesus and Milton both kept first things first. Do the best job of producing what everyone craves.

Reflection

The Best Evangelism Is Transformed Lives

Dallas Willard makes a compelling case that authentic transformation (Christian spiritual formation) should be the primary mission of each local congregation. The best way to do *outreach* is to do an outstanding job of *inreach*—the renovation of hearts that turns people, wherever they are, into lights in a darkened world.

If making a quality kiss of chocolate got the attention of the world, without advertising crusades, just imagine what making quality Christians would do. After all, who *doesn't* enjoy the experience of love, peace, and joy?

I was discussing a formational approach to evangelism last week with a pretty high-powered group of pastors who concentrate their efforts on reaching out to those who've been hurt by the church. One of the pastors had been meeting with a group of twentysomethings who had been gathering in his office to air out their anger for the established church. Because of the pastor's busy schedule, the group would often be together in the outer office, sipping coffee, before the meeting began. There they would have the occasion to interact with Faye, the pastor's fiftysomething secretary, each week.

Last week as the group was settling in the pastor's office, a young man with prominent tattoos and a variety of pierced body parts announced, "If hanging out with Jesus can make me as happy and caring as Faye, I want in. I want what she's got."

No spiritual laws were read, no magic questions were asked, but Faye had taken a page from Milton Hershey's playbook. She had created something that everyone wants. The best way to sell chocolate is to make the best chocolate. The best way to apprentice others is to be a passionate apprentice.

Apprentice Activity
A Final Assessment

Take a few moments to complete the following exercise. It's a self-assessment concerning what Dallas calls "God's Plan for Spiritual Formation." Think about your experience with the apprentice activities before responding.

Step 1: Disciples (or apprentices of Jesus) are with him, learning to be like him.

Give an example of a special way you have begun spending time with Jesus each day over the past 30 days, and describe how this is helping you become more like him.

_____

_____

_____

_____

_____

Step 2: Apprentices are being immersed at all levels of growth in the Trinitarian presence. (Growth in experience of Trinity means we have more of an experiential awareness of God as creator, teacher, and healer. Being immersed in this community of love also takes away the need to perform—to do things to win the approval of the raters and grade givers of the world.)

What are some ways in which you *experience* God as your Father, teacher, and healer?

_____

_____

_____

_____

_____

Have you noticed that this experience of the community of love (the Trinitarian presence of God) is freeing you from a sense of needing to perform in order to prove your value or worth? How so?

_____

_____

_____

_____

_____

Step 3: Apprentices are becoming transformed inwardly in such a way that doing the words and deeds of Christ is not the focus but is becoming the natural outcome of community life. That is, disciples begin to act like Christ because they are *becoming* like him—as opposed to *acting* like him through the power of human will.

When it comes to doing the "words and deeds" of Christ, does it feel more like you are "eating your vegetables" or opening a box of chocolates? Why so?

_____

_____

_____

_____

_____

Simmering in Colossians 3:1–17 Continued. Please slowly reread verses 1–15 and then meditatively ponder verses 16 and 17:

Let the word of Christ dwell in you richly; teach and admonish one another in all wisdom; and with gratitude in your hearts sing psalms, hymns, and spiritual songs to God. And whatever you do, in word or deed, do everything in the name of the Lord Jesus, giving thanks to God the Father through him.

Now What?

The Ongoing Mystical Experience of Theology

I n the preceding pages, I've suggested the need for programs of discipleship that resemble both a medieval apprenticeship and the method of formation Jesus used with his disciples. I've made this case because the word *discipleship* has not aged well—particularly as used by modern-day evangelicals. What is missing is the experience of theology through living a "with-God" life.

In his book *Russian Mystics*, Sergius Bolshakoff offers the following observation:

> Once theology and mysticism start to drift apart, the former tends invariably to become a "theology of concepts," an abstract science, a mere religious philosophy. Those who teach theology cease to live up to it as the mystics did.
>
> In order to return to the great age of theology, dogma must be brought back to life and mystically experienced.[1]

I believe this "drift," or "regression to the mean" if you will, is as much a part of the spiritual history of the church as

239

are the great revival movements. In fact, I would suggest that much of church history reflects a series of sinusoidal waves, great peaks of experiencing life with God (e.g., the fervor of the early church, monastic movements, monastic movement reforms, the Reformation, Wesleyan Holiness revivals, the Keswick Movement, the modern charismatic renewal) always followed by a return to "normal" living. Souls become molten in the presence of God—as they *experience* God. Souls cool and congeal as theology and mysticism begin to drift apart.

It may seem that I've picked on evangelicals. That was not my intent. In fact, I believe that when the language of evangelicalism first originated in sixteenth-century Germany—think Martin Luther—it was because of the growing fervor over the "Evangels," the Gospels and their application to life. The first "evangelicals" were meeting Jesus for themselves through reading the Gospel accounts. As Dallas Willard points out, "What lay at the heart of evangelical religion at its origin? Two things: (1) devotion to the Bible as the ultimate source of authority and divine life, and (2) personal experience of conversion to and practical communion with God."[2]

Sadly, the experience of conversion as living in practical communion with God has become lost to most modern-day expressions of evangelicalism. For many, salvation has become synonymous with the forgiveness of sins and discipleship has focused on learning facts about the Bible and denominational distinctives. And it has been during this most recent trough—this deep valley in the spiritual history of the church—that the modern spiritual formation movement has been birthed.

I believe the massive amount of recent attention given to "spiritual formation" is because of a deep desire for the experience of God not offered by modern evangelicalism. In discussions of spiritual formation, terms such as *salvation* are being re-visioned in more comprehensive and relational terms—John 17:3 terms. As was the case with the early church, modern Christians are coming to see salvation as more than a "get out of hell free" card. Salvation is participation in a transforming friendship with God, here and now. And with this new/old view of salvation, discipleship is coming to be seen more and more in terms of entering into apprenticeship with the risen Lord. Discipleship is the journey with God through which spiritual (trans)formation occurs.

So now what?

The practice of an apprenticeship with Jesus means waking up each morning with the primary purpose of being with Christ while learning to be like him. It is learning to live more and more moments in awareness of the Trinitarian reality, the kingdom of God all around. So, if any of the apprenticeship activities in this book were helpful, great. Let a few become recurring reminders in your Outlook program—or simply jot them down in your prayer journal. If spending time with others who are farther down the path helps, great; be more intentional about spending time with these "spiritual directors."

But the main thing is not what to do but what not to do. We should not make entering into an apprenticeship with Jesus complicated. If you will indulge me for one last Dallasism—one I like to refer to as Dallas 3:16—in response to the question, "How does a person become a saint?" he said, "By doing the next right thing." I don't think he will mind if we tweak this slightly and offer the suggestion, how does a person become an apprentice of Jesus? By doing the next right thing with him, until eventually you observe him doing the next right thing through you.

Appendix

If you would like to use some of the daily exercises in this book to build an "E-Rule of Life," the following screenshots are presented to help you with that process. While step-by-step notes are given in the text, the visuals in this appendix are provided to help you to know that you are on the right track.

It is my fondest hope that when you complete *Apprenticeship with Jesus*, you will have also constructed an "E-Rule" of daily, weekly, and monthly prompts as an ongoing reminder for living more and more moments of your life "with God."

Table 1
Sleep 8 Hours–Recurring Appointment

Table 2
Schedule Time with God

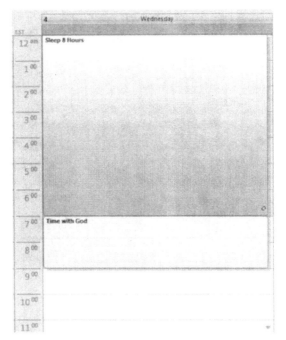

Table 3
Two-Hour Block

Table 4
Shorter Blocks of Time

4	Wednesday
EST	
12 am	Sleep 8 Hours
1 00	
2 00	
3 00	
4 00	
5 00	
6 00	
7 00	Time with God / Time With God
8 00	
9 00	Time With God
10 00	
11 00	Time with God

Table 5
12 Steps of Repentance–Task

Due every day effective 3/1/2009.

Subject: 12 Steps of Repentance

Start date:	None	Status:	In Progress
Due date:	None	Priority: High	% Complete: 0%

☑ Reminder: Sun 3/1/2009   7:00 AM   Owner: Rich Cannon

1. *I admit that I am powerless to fix the brokenness of my life on my own. My life has become unmanageable.*

2. *I believe that God—through his actions and those of his son Jesus and the Holy Spirit—can restore me to sanity.*

3. *I will turn my will and my entire life over to the care of God. Father, I'm asking for a total transfusion of your will, power, presence and love.*

4. **I will make a searching and fearless inventory of my life to discover all the ways I have engaged in self-worship (by being in control instead of living surrendered to the will of God).**

5. **I will admit to God, to myself, and to another human being the exact nature of my wrongs.**

6. **I am entirely ready to have God remove all the defects in my character and replace them—through his presence—with the thoughts, emotions, will, behavior, and relationship patterns of Christ.**

7. **I humbly ask God to help me become willing to deny myself—and the desire to live life on my terms—and to remove my shortcomings.**

8. **I will make a list of all the people I have harmed and become willing to make amends.**

Contacts...

Table 6
Creating a One-Time-Per-Day Prompt

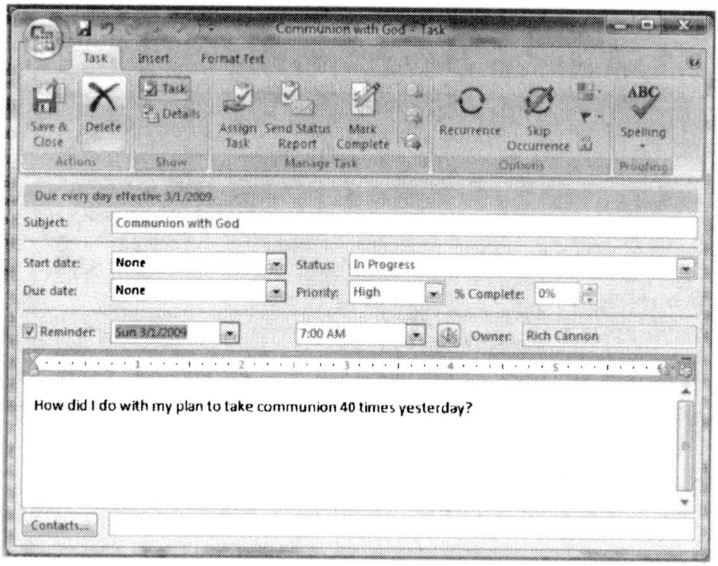

Table 7
Scripture Plan Prompt

So if you have been raised with Christ, seek the things that are above, where Christ is, seated at the right hand of God. Set your minds on things that are above, not on things that are on earth, for you have died and your life is hidden with Christ in God.

[1]So if you have been raised with Christ, seek the things that are above, where Christ is, seated at the right hand of God.

[2]Set your minds on things that are above, not on things that are on earth,

[3]for you have died, and your life is hidden with Christ in God.

[4]When Christ who is your life is revealed, then you also will be revealed with him in glory.

[5]Put to death, therefore, whatever in you is earthly: fornication, impurity, passion, evil desire, and greed (which is idolatry).

[6]On account of these the wrath of God is coming on those who are disobedient.

[7]These are the ways you also once followed, when you were living that life.

[8]But now you must get rid of all such things—anger, wrath, malice, slander, and abusive language from your mouth.

[9]Do not lie to one another, seeing that you have stripped off the old self with its practices

[10]and have clothed yourselves with the new self, which is being renewed in knowledge according to the image of its creator.

[11]In that renewal there is no longer Greek and Jew, circumcised and uncircumcised, barbarian, Scythian, slave and free; but Christ is all and in all!

[12]As God's chosen ones, holy and beloved, clothe yourselves with compassion, kindness, humility, meekness, and patience.

[13]Bear with one another and, if anyone has a complaint against another, forgive each other; just as the Lord has forgiven you, so you also must forgive.

[14]Above all, clothe yourselves with love, which binds everything together in perfect harmony.

[15]And let the peace of Christ rule in your hearts, to which indeed you were called in the one body. And be thankful.

[16]Let the word of Christ dwell in you richly; teach and admonish one another in all wisdom; and with gratitude in your hearts sing psalms, hymns, and spiritual songs to God.

[17]And whatever you do, in word or deed, do everything in the name of the Lord Jesus, giving thanks to God the Father through him.

Notes

Introduction

1. David Kinnaman and Gabe Lyons, *unChristian: What a New Generation Really Thinks about Christianity . . . and Why It Matters* (Grand Rapids: Baker, 2007).

2. Dallas Willard, *The Spirit of the Disciplines: Understanding How God Changes Lives* (San Francisco: HarperCollins, 1991), ix.

3. Dallas Willard, *The Divine Conspiracy: Rediscovering Our Hidden Life in God* (San Francisco: HarperCollins, 1998), 86.

4. See Barbara A. Hanawalt, *Growing Up in Medieval London: The Experience of Childhood in History* (New York: Oxford University Press, 1995), 129.

5. Ibid., 135.

Getting Started

1. This story was originally told to me by Mark Walker and is included here by permission.

Day 1: A Case of Theological Malpractice

1. For an extended quote, see Dallas Willard, *The Great Omission: Reclaiming Jesus' Essential Teaching of Discipleship* (San Francisco: HarperCollins, 2006), 65: "If there is anything we should know by now it is that a gospel of justification alone does not generate disciples. Discipleship is a life of learning from Jesus Christ how to live in the Kingdom of God now, as he himself did. If you want to be a person of grace, then, live a holy life of discipleship, because the only way you can do that is on a steady diet of grace. Works of the Kingdom live from grace."

2. Ibid., 52.

3. I am thinking of books such as *Letters of a Modern Mystic* by Frank C. Laubach, *A Testament of Devotion* by Thomas R. Kelly, *Markings* by Dag Hammarskjold, *Practicing the Presence* by Brother Lawrence, and *A Confession* by Leo Tolstoy.

4. Eugene Peterson, *The Contemplative Pastor* (Grand Rapids: Eerdmans, 1989), 18.

5. Ibid., 23.

Day 2: Getting Beyond Vampire Christianity

1. For a compelling overview, please see Ronald J. Sider, *The Scandal of the Evangelical Conscience: Why Are Christians Living Just Like the Rest of the World* (Grand Rapids: Baker, 2005).

Day 3: Why Paul Rarely Quoted Jesus

1. Huston Smith, *The World's Religions* (San Francisco: HarperSanFrancisco, 1991), 330.

2. Ibid.

3. Lewis B. Smedes, *Union with Christ: A Biblical View of the New Life in Jesus Christ*, 2nd rev. ed. (Grand Rapids: Eerdmans, 1983).

4. I'm thinking in particular of some of the arguments found in *The Divine Conspiracy* by Dallas Willard and *A Generous Orthodoxy* by Brian McLaren.

Day 4: Becoming Odd for God

1. Class notes from "Spirituality and Ministry," June 4–15, 2007. Fuller Seminary. Mater Dolorosa Retreat Center. Dallas Willard and Keith Mathews, Instructors.

2. See Revelation 20:6.

Meet the Master

1. Barbara A. Hanawalt, *Growing Up in Medieval London: The Experience of Childhood in History* (New York: Oxford University Press, 1995), 135.

Day 5: Desiring to Dance with the Trinity

1. Kalistos Ware, *The Orthodox Way* (Crestwood, NY: St. Vladimir's Seminary Press, 1995), 89.

2. This point is made and developed in Darrell W. Johnson, *Experiencing the Trinity* (Vancouver: Regent College, 2004), 32. Johnson attributes the specific insight to Thomas Torrance in *Trinitarian Perspectives: Toward Doctrinal Agreement* (Edinburgh: T&T Clark, 1994), 1. However, Johnson goes on to develop this insight in a manner that is both fresh and deeply moving.

Day 7: Emulating the Master's Creativity

1. See discussion on creation found in Wayne Grudem, *Bible Doctrine: Essential Teachings of the Christian Faith* (Grand Rapids: Zondervan, 1999).

Day 8: Tapping into the Force

1. Many people argue that, given enough time, even the most improbable events become probable. This sounds reasonable only until specific numbers are used. Let's consider George Bernard Shaw's argument that if a million monkeys constantly typed on a million typewriters for a long enough time, one of them would eventually pound out a Shakespearean play. Assume a million monkeys typing 24 hours a day at 100 words a minute on typewriters with 40 keys. If each word of the play contained four letters, the first word would be typed by one of the monkeys in about 12 seconds. However, it would require about five days to get the first two words (eight letters) on one of the typewriters. How long would it take to get the first four words? About 100 billion years! No one could imagine the amount of time that

would be required to produce the first scene. (From Ken Boa and Larry Moody, *I'm Glad You Asked* [Colorado Springs: David C. Cook, 1995], 43–44).

Know Yourself

1. Hanawalt, *Growing Up in Medieval London*, 129.
2. Ibid., 164.
3. You may want to see Rob Bell's video, *Dust*, which is part of his Nooma series. See also: http://www.offqueue .com/archives/dust_rabbi.pdf.
4. Ibid.

Day 9: The Good

1. The First Council of Nicaea in 325 debated the terms *homoousios* and *homoiousios*. The word *homoousios* means "same substance," whereas the word *homoiousios* means "similar substance." The council affirmed the Father, Son, and Holy Spirit (Godhead) are of the *homoousious* (same substance). Many commentators—most notably Walter Gibbon—have noted that the entire controversy hung on a difference of the smallest Greek letter (*i*, or iota).
2. C. S. Lewis, *The Weight of Glory: And Other Addresses* (New York: HarperCollins, 1949/2001), 46.

Day 10: The Bad

1. C. S. Lewis, *Mere Christianity* (San Francisco: HarperSanFrancisco, 1952/2001), 200.
2. Dallas Willard, *The Divine Conspiracy: Rediscovering Our Hidden Life in God* (San Francisco: HarperCollins, 1998), 42.
3. http://www.christianitytoday.com/bc/2005/001/3.8.html. And as Ron Sider goes on to underscore in this book *The Scandal of the Evangelical Conscience: Why Are Christians Living Just Like the Rest of the World?* (Grand Rapids: Baker, 2005), the problem is not limited to South Africa. The bottom line is, it is almost impossible to actually become like Jesus, to do the one and only thing that Christianity is about. Why?
4. Willard, *Divine Conspiracy*, 51.

Day 11: The Ugly

1. Anthony A. Hoekema, *Created in God's Image* (Grand Rapids: Eerdmans, 1986), ix.

Day 12: The Beautiful

1. Spoiler warning! If you have not seen *16 Blocks*, what you are about to read may spoil some of the surprises. So, Bruce Willis and I would like to invite you to go rent the DVD before continuing with this chapter.

Ways of Being with the Master

1. See Dallas Willard's article "Discipleship" in *The Oxford Handbook of Evangelical Theology*, ed. Gerald McDermott (New York: Oxford University Press, forthcoming 2010).

Day 13: Life Is Too Long

1. Part of the human potential movement, the purpose of the highly controversial Erhard Seminars Training (est) was personal empowerment and life transformation.
2. A. W. Tozer, *The Pursuit of God* (Harrisburg, PA: Christian Publications, Inc., 1982), 13.

Day 16: Baptized into a Whole New Way to Live

1. http://www.hollywoodjesus.com/Apostle.htm.
2. Ibid.

Day 17: Getting Scripture All the Way through Me

1. Brian McLaren, *A New Kind of Christian* (San Francisco: Jossey-Bass, 2001), 56.

2. See Dallas Willard's article "Discipleship" in *The Oxford Handbook of Evangelical Theology*, ed. Gerald McDermott (New York: Oxford University Press, forthcoming 2010).

Day 18: A "With-God" Approach to Scripture

1. Richard J. Foster, et al., ed. *The Renovaré Spiritual Formation Bible* (San Francisco: HarperSanFrancisco, 2005), xxv.

2. Ibid., xxvii.

Day 20: Meditation and Monk Fights

1. 1 Cor. 12:12, 27 NRSV.

2. http://www.trappist.net/newweb/directions.html.

Day 21: The Solace of Solitude

1. Henri J. M. Nouwen, *Out of Solitude: Three Meditations on the Christian Life* (Notre Dame: Ave Maria Press, 1974/2008; rev. 2004), 18, 26.

2. James A. Connor, *Silent Fire: Bringing the Spirituality of Silence into Everyday Life* (New York: Crown, 2002), 203.

Day 22: If God Is So Smart, Why Am I Doing All the Talking?

1. Dallas Willard, *Hearing God: Developing a Conversational Relationship with God* (Downers Grove, IL: InterVarsity, 1999), 18.

2. Ibid., 10. Also see Exodus 29:42–46; 33:11; Psalm 23; Isaiah 41:8; John 15:14; and Hebrews 13:5–6.

3. Ibid., 148 (emphasis mine).

4. Ibid., 152 (emphasis mine).

Carrying On the Master's Legacy

1. Willard, *Hearing God*, 139.

Day 25: Getting through the Rough Spots

1. Dallas Willard, *Renovation of the Heart: Putting on the Character of Christ* (Colorado Springs: NavPress, 2002), 85.

2. Gary Moon, *Falling for God* (Colorado Springs: Shaw, 2004), 140.

3. John Calvin, *Institutes*, Book III, ch. 7.

Day 26: Working with the Proper Light

1. From the song "Anthem" on the album *The Future* by Leonard Cohen.

Day 27: The Need to Slow Down

1. Class notes from "Spirituality and Ministry," June 4–15, 2007. Fuller Seminary. Mater Dolorosa Retreat Center. Dallas Willard and Keith Mathews, Instructors.

Day 28: Eating a Balanced Diet

1. Gary W. Moon. *Participant's Guide: Streams of Living Water: Celebrating the Great Traditions of Christian Faith* (Franklin Springs: LifeSprings, 2007), 22.

2. Ibid., 59.

3. Ibid., 76.

4. Ibid., 94.

5. Ibid., 113.

Day 29: Becoming a Master Craftsman

1. C. S. Lewis, *Mere Christianity* (San Francisco: HarperSanFrancisco, 1952/2001), 200.

2. Dallas Willard, *Renovation of the Heart: Putting on the Character of Christ* (Colorado Springs: NavPress, 2002). See also the DVD-based small group curriculum by LifeSprings, http://www.lifespringsresources.com/store/products/filter.aspx?filter=Elective&Category=Renovation+of+the+Heart.

Now What?

1. Sergius Bolshakoff, *Russian Mystics* (Kalamazoo, MI: Cistercian Publications, 1976), xx.

2. See Dallas Willard's article "Discipleship" in *The Oxford Handbook of Evangelical Theology*, ed. Gerald McDermott (New York: Oxford University Press, forthcoming 2010).

Gary W. Moon (MDiv, PhD) is Vice-President and Chair of Integration at Richmont Graduate University—formerly Psychological Studies Institute. He also serves as the executive director of the Renovaré International Institute for Christian Spiritual Formation.

He received his BA and MA from the University of Georgia and MDiv and PhD in clinical psychology from Fuller Theological Seminary. He is a licensed psychologist in Georgia and Virginia.

Moon serves on the editorial boards of *The Journal of Psychology and Christianity*, *The Journal Psychology*, and *Theology, Marriage and Family: A Christian Journal*. He along with David Benner and Larry Crabb serve as executive editors for *Conversations: A Forum for Authentic Transformation*.

He conducts research concerning the theoretical and practical integration of psychology and theology and has published or presented over 100 professional and popular papers.

His most recent books include *Falling for God* (Shaw/Random House, 2004) and *Spiritual Direction and the Care of Souls* (IVP, 2004). Other books include *Homesick for Eden* (Servant, 1997) and a four-volume family devotion series, The Bible Ride (Servant and LifeSprings).

Through Richmont and LifeSprings he has developed a DVD-based curriculum of Christlikeness series for small groups based on the work of Curt Cloninger (*God Views*), Dallas Willard (*Renovation of the Heart*), and Richard J. Foster (*Celebration of Discipline* and *Streams of Living Water*).

The RENOVARÉ International Institute for Christian Spiritual Formation

A TWO-YEAR EXPERIENCE OF BECOMING LIKE JESUS

"The spiritual formation field lacks intellectual rigor and testable information needed to put the gospel and spiritual life in Christ on the cognitive map for the multitudes of people who are hungry for something real."

— *Dallas Willard*

YOUR FACULTY